DC GOD LOL?

**Compiled and edited by
Frankie Mulgrew**

To Peter + Jacinta,

God bless lots,

Fr Frankie

DARTON·LONGMAN+TODD

To Dad
*for introducing me to one of
God's greatest gifts*

First published in 2013 by
Darton, Longman and Todd Ltd
1 Spencer Court
140 – 142 Wandsworth High Street
London SW18 4JJ

All royalties from the sale of this work will be donated to the charity
Mary's Meals

ISBN 978-0-232-53003-2

A catalogue record for this book is available from the British Library.

Printed and bound by Bell & Bain, Glasgow

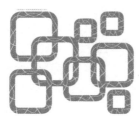

The human race has only one really effective weapon, and that is laughter. The moment it arises, all your irritations and resentments slip away and the sunny spirit takes their place.

Mark Twain

God made us for joy. God is joy, and the joy of living reflects the original joy that God felt in creating us.

Blessed John Paul II

You will teach me the path of life, unbounded joy in your presence, at your right hand delight forever.

Psalm 16:11

ROBERT DUNCAN

CONTENTS

A THANK YOU FROM MARY'S MEALS

Does God LOL? will undoubtedly bring a smile to the faces of those who read it but, since a portion of the proceeds will be donated to Mary's Meals, sales of the book will also mean that many children – who would otherwise be working, begging or even foraging for their next meal – will be sitting in a classroom with a full stomach, learning how to read and write. Thank you to the book's contributors, publishers and readers for joining the many people all over the world who will not accept that any child in this world of plenty must endure a day without a meal.

Find out more about the excellent work of Mary's Meals on page 143.

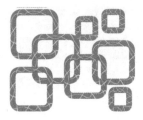

ACKNOWLEDGEMENTS

This book would not have been possible without the generosity, kindness and support of the contributors ... and a few others: David Moloney, Magnus MacFarlane-Barrow, Father Peter Cullen, Helen Porter, Kevin Mayhew, Anne Jones, Rita Tomlinson, Father Lee Marshall, Father Dan Fitzpatrick, John Pridmore, Dale Mulgrew, Jamie Mulgrew, Chris Gidney, Father Phillip Caldwell, Father Kieran Fletcher, Frances Henley Lock, Father John Udris, Lord David Alton, David Wells, Barbara Mason, Rosanne Walker.

FOREWORD – GOD AND HUMOUR

TOM WRIGHT

If you want evidence that God has a sense of humour, the fact that Frankie Mulgrew has invited me to write a foreword to this book ought to be enough. People often make jokes about bishops, but most people don't expect the bishops to see the funny side, let alone come up with a few good lines themselves.

Unless, of course, you go back to Christianity's Jewish roots, as we should. Plenty of good stuff there. 'The good news,' says Moses to the Israelites, 'is that we've got the commandments down from forty to ten; the bad news is that adultery is still in.'

Jewish humour, like the humour of my native Tyneside, is often born out of desperation. When things are bad, the only way to survive is to see the funny side. A friend was telling me about how he'd injured himself doing something at home but managed to drive himself to the hospital; then, in the car park, he opened the car door and another car smashed into it. 'I sometimes think,' he said, 'that if I didn't have bad luck I wouldn't have any luck at all.' That may for all I know be an old line, but it was still a good one.

I suspect that several of Jesus's remarks, once we get

behind the solemn face we put on in church, were meant to be like that. A camel going through the eye of a needle? Someone with a plank of wood in his eye? It's all in the timing, which is what you usually don't get in church.

Or, if you do, it's often an accident. My father used to read the lessons in church and sometimes he'd practice them at home beforehand. One day, rehearsing, he announced that the Second Lesson was taken from the Epistle of Paul the Colossal . . . my sister and I were willing him to repeat that in church (and see if anyone noticed), but sadly he kept his nerve and got it right. There are plenty of other examples of the same kind of thing in this book.

Then there are times when the Bible quite accidentally gives you the one-liner you need for a particular moment. A close friend of mine managed not to get married until he turned 50, and he asked me to preach at his wedding. He and his bride chose the reading about Jesus turning water into wine at Cana, where Mary tells Jesus the wine has run out and Jesus says, 'Woman, what have you to do with me? My hour has not yet come.' (Then he does the water/wine thing anyway.) So I stared at this reading and realised I'd struck gold. What an appropriate reading it was, I said. Michael here has spent the last 50 years of his life saying 'Woman, what have you to do with me? My hour has not yet come.'

Actually, the whole Bible is full of humour, not just the accidental type when people get the words wrong. There is a wonderful passage in Genesis (chapter 14) which lists a lot of unpronounceable kings and their countries and describes them making war on each other. Then, as they are charging about the place, a lot of them fall into bitumen pits. Try reading it out loud in church, and unless people are in stitches by the end they haven't seen the point – which is partly that God looks down on all the stupid pomp and circumstance that petty humans get up to, and lets them wallow in the result.

You get the same thing in Daniel 3, which lists all the self-important Babylonian officials – the satraps, the prefects, the governors, the counsellors, the treasurers, the justices, the magistrates, and all the provincial officials – and then repeats the list, making them sound even more like something out of a Gilbert and Sullivan opera. Then the king announces that everyone has to bow down and worship a golden statue 'when they hear the sound of the horn, pipe, lyre, trigon, harp, drum, and entire musical ensemble' – a list of instruments which is repeated four times. We are meant to get the sense of an entire system puffed up full with hot air, waiting for someone (Daniel and his friends) to come along with a little pin. The explosion, when it comes, is deadly serious, but the slapstick side of it is part of the point.

Sometimes we can play the same trick ourselves – the build-up of pomp and circumstance and then the one-line put-down. I had to preach before a cathedral full of judges and lawyers, all wigs and robes and what-have-you. I began with the old line about four different European systems, and added a twist. You know: in France everything is permitted except that which is forbidden; in Italy everything is permitted including that which is

forbidden; in Germany everything is forbidden except
that which is permitted; in Russia everything is forbidden
including that which is permitted. Then the new twist: In
Britain we know that everything is either permitted or
forbidden, but we're not sure which is which because
we're waiting for a decision from the European Court.

We ought to expect humour in the Bible, because the
Bible tells the story of how all of life has somehow got
out of joint, has become absurd, and how the God who
made it in the first place has come into the middle of it
to sort it all out. Humour is what happens when things
come together incongruously. Humour, in fact, is a sign
that we all know in our bones that something is wrong
somewhere, at quite a deep level. The Bible is about God
coming into the middle of that incongruous, out-of-joint
world. Incarnation and new creation are bound to be
funny, and if we don't see it we aren't tuned in. Hence
Jesus' mixture of stand-up comedy and street theatre
(which we miss because we think of him making solemn
pronouncements from a pulpit).

Of course, God's coming into the world is desperately sad as well. There is nothing funny about Jesus's
crucifixion. However, tears and laughter, as some of the
contributors to this book point out, are very close. They
are part of the clue to being genuinely human. Animals
don't laugh or cry (hyenas and crocodiles only appear
to be doing so, they aren't really). Nor do computers.
Nor do computers hug you, or forgive you, or pat you
on the back. Tears and laughter are key ways in which we
humans remind ourselves, and one another, that life is

out of joint, and that it's okay to recognise it. And to stop ourselves taking ourselves too seriously. That we are, in fact, humans, creatures, messed-up creatures at that, but still greatly loved by our creator.

Tears and laughter, though, are not direct equivalents. The Book of Revelation tells us that in the New Jerusalem God himself will wipe away all tears from everyone's eyes. It doesn't say that God will abolish laughter. Why, the biggest joke will be that we are there ourselves. 'Didn't expect that, did you?' – as the bishop said to the actress.

DR N.T. (TOM) WRIGHT, formerly Bishop of Durham, is now Professor of New Testament and Early Christianity at the University of St Andrews.

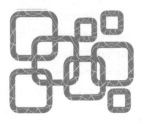

There is hope for the future because God has a sense of humor and we are funny to God.

Bill Cosby

Joy is the serious business of heaven.

C. S. Lewis

These I shall lead to my holy mountain and make them joyful in my house of prayer.

Isaiah 56:7

INTRODUCTION

FRANKIE MULGREW

There is a true story about a young man with cerebral palsy who was a Catholic, but because of his condition, whenever the time came for him to receive Holy Communion he could not open his mouth. The priest realised the only way he could get him to open his mouth was to tell him a joke and make him laugh, and while he was laughing the priest was able to give him Communion. I love that story, because it tells us that God came to him in such a sacred moment through the aid of laughter and joy. A recurring theme throughout the Scriptures is that those who have God have joy! An evidential sign that any person from the Bible has the Spirit of God within them is great joy matched with inner peace. Regardless of ever-changing circumstances around them, they have an underlying peace and joy that no person, place or thing can take away from them! And I would have to agree, that has certainly been my experience as a former sufferer of depression. I'll tell you how bad my depression was … I used to watch episodes of *EastEnders* as an anti-depressant.

Jesus said himself he had come to give life in abundance (John 10:10). Surely abundant life is not possible if you celebrate all the attributes of being human but leave out smiling and laughter. Jesus kept going round telling everyone the kingdom of God was like a fantastic wedding feast … and since the kingdom of God was now already present, it was time to start celebrating![1]

You see, in the Our Father we have the line 'your will be done on earth as it is in heaven'. From the advent of Jesus and ever since, the Kingdom of heaven has been breaking into the world, becoming more and more present, depending on how open we are to it. It is revealing itself bit by bit. We see this, in glimpses of heaven on earth, glimpses of things now on earth as they will be for all time in heaven, like acts of love, kindness, and so on. [2] It is my belief that when we laugh, from an innocent and integral source, that laughter is a glimpse on earth of the happiness we will feel for all time in eternity.

It says in John's letter 'God is love' (1 John 4:8). And when you unpack that what does it mean? God wills us well! God wants the best for us. An evident sign of this love, a willing well, must be in emotions and feelings of happiness and joy. Can you imagine a romantic candlelit dinner as a man gets down on one knee, produces a ring and proposes to his girlfriend: 'Will you marry me? wait, hold on … don't smile you're ruining it!' A smile, a laugh, is a term of affection of how we let others know we appreciate them. Similarly imagine the scene, a surprise birthday party, the birthday guy or gal turns

1. Jean Vanier in G.A. Arbuckle, *Laughing with God* (Liturgical Press, 2008), p. ix.
2. Timothy Radcliffe, talk given at Newcastle City Hall, 2006.

on the lights to reveal all those near and dear to them shouting 'Surprise!' The birthday person, with exuberant joy welling up, bursts out into spontaneous laughter. The organiser immediately stops everything, turns off the music and announces 'Wait! Are you laughing ... you're not taking this seriously. Right! Everybody out!'

A comedian similarly – dare I say it – wills you well... s/he want you to be happier, certainly happier then when you first came into the gig. I'm yet to meet a comedian who has found out that there is someone in the audience with a terminal illness or who has just suffered a bereave-ment and does not want to go out and entertain them. Far from it, they want to give them a great night.

In the film *Bruce Almighty*, Morgan Freeman as God, puts his arm round Jim Carrey's character and tells him 'You have a divine spark! You have a gift for bringing joy and laughter into the world ... I know, I created you.' That's fundamentally what a comedian is – someone who brings laughter and joy into the world. I saw a famous comedian on a chat show once referring to his job as a vocation ... a calling ... just like a call to the priesthood. It certainly is a special role for our times.

And that's where the inspiration for this book came from, exploring where this gift, all this laughter, and the ability to create happiness comes from. It's not a book written by theologians and philosophers – that's been done. It's by foot soldiers, on the ground laughter-makers, sharing thoughts and reflections on how they see God's sense of humour. Some will be funny, some light, serious, deep, inspiring, zany, insightful, etc. You might disagree with some points, and that's okay as they are sharing their personal perspectives. But the hope is that we will get nearer to understanding God's humour through his different faces in the world. And so, along with written contributions, some of the inputs in the book have been done via interviews.

So here are the champions of this book, providing laughter through social, cultural and political change. Through people's highs and lows these are the merry who just want to bring a little bit of joy into our lives. These contributors have made sacrifices and have known misfortune themselves – that's what makes them experts at joking about it. They wish you well, have a desire to give you a lift and help ease your burdens. So, from these different perspectives we try to understand God's sense of humour – from the ideas, thoughts and inspiration of those who spend their lives promoting humour in our world!

And, if at all possible, if there was one thing I'd like you to take away from the book, it would be this – hope. Hope in a God of laughter!

DOES GOD HAVE A SENSE OF HUMOUR?

TIM VINE

Yes. The end.

Does God have a sense of humour! Of course he does. I could give you a thousand examples just from the animal kingdom. Look at a camel's face, or a llama walking away from you, listen to a chicken clucking or a mynah bird imitating your granny asking for a cup of tea. Watch a line of ducklings trying to keep up with their mother. Animals can be very funny. Admittedly you wouldn't know it if you watched an episode of America's *Animals Do the Funniest Things,* but that's not the point. That's because some people don't know how to make television shows. What I mean is, spend some time in an animal's company and they'll make you laugh. I don't suggest you take an ostrich to the cinema though because they'll have your popcorn and there's nothing amusing about that. The point is there are too many funny animals for it not to have been part of the plan. When it comes to animals, assuming you believe God made them, the evidence is that God wanted animals to be majestic, intricate, awe inspiring, extraordinary, and yes, at times funny. And if someone wants something to be funny then that person has a sense of humour.

And what about us? Is there any evidence in mankind that God wants to make us laugh? Well, I believe there is one very obvious sign that God wants us all to laugh. It's called laughter.

Laughter exists so that we can all react accordingly after something funny happens. That's what it's for. Laughter doesn't have any other function. It has lots of beneficial side effects but that isn't why it's there. You never hear someone say, 'I'm running a little low on endorphins so if you'll excuse me I'm just going to have a bit of a laugh into my hankie'. Eyes are used for seeing, lungs are used for breathing, and laughter is used when you find something funny. Do you think God would have invented ears in a totally silent world? Of course not. We have ears because there are sounds to hear, so surely it follows that we have laughter because there are laughs to be had.

Yes, Tim, I hear you say mischievously, that's all very rosy and lovely, but taking that line of logic could one not also argue that God wants us to be sad because he also invented crying? Well, in the words of the boy sitting next to me in my maths O level exam, 'I don't have all the answers.' Perhaps God's original design for crying was that it was something that happened during excessive laughter, I don't know. I do know that in this world when problems come and sadness and suffering are suddenly part of your life it is the time spent with friends and family that so often pulls people through. And if you think of your fondest memories of friends and family, I bet most of them involve laughter. God knew it would be thus.

I believe God has a sense of humour because he created laughter. And what an invention it was! You can enjoy it in almost any situation. (I don't advise funerals.) However there is one question that continues to bug me: Which came first? Laughter or the camel's face?

TIM VINE is a comedian, writer and actor who once held the world record for the most jokes told in an hour. He has starred in the BAFTA award-winning *The Sketch Show*, and the sitcom *Not Going Out* along with appearing regularly on our TV screens in numerous shows, including *Live at the Apollo* and the Royal Variety Performance.

THE GIFT

RICKY TOMLINSON

There was a friend of ours called Joey Rogers. Joey was a great country and western singer and a lovely, wonderful, human being. He could have made the big time on the country scene but he just used to play around the pubs. The singer Charlie Landsborough was a big fan of this guy, I mean everyone loved Joey Rogers. Anyway he died and his funeral was in Christ and King, the big Catholic church on the drive, and the priest was this stocky Irish lad. The Church was packed and there were hundreds of people outside. They played the music and we all sat down. The priest got up and he went 'It's wonderful to see so many people here paying their last respects to Joey, obviously he was a very, very popular man and well loved by everyone … and of course he was well known for his country music.' And then he said, 'I didn't realise how much country and western music meant to me until my dog died.' I thought that was wonderful; the place went up, and I thought that's great, everyone's having a laugh, because Joey Rogers would have been roaring laughing … even in death! And I bet God was laughing. I mean what could be better than if you're in Church and you're listening to a sermon and the vicar or the priest tells a few gags. I think that would be great, it would lighten up the whole service.

God must have a sense of humour, he would have to, to have put up with me and some of my harebrained schemes. He's obviously got to have a sense of humour and I'm sure he can take a good joke about himself. I don't think there's any problem there, no problem whatsoever. I think God gives us the power to laugh and the power and intelligence to make things funny and to be funny.

I just think there's so much beauty around us that he's got to be a fun person, he has to be a lovely, lovely person. You know when you go to the Lake District and you see the wonderful sights (we've been lucky we've travelled all over the place), and there are some wonderful sights. So he must be a lovely person and a lovely being and so if he's a lovely being he must have this wonderful sense of humour. We know he's full of compassion and we know he's full of care and tenderness, we know that. So I don't think he could be anything other than full of fun and humour, you would have to have that sort of spirit in you to make wonderful trees, ravines, oceans, mountains, lakes, wonderful land animals and plants. You would have to be on a high to do that, you would have to have that feeling of wellbeing and that's what being funny is, a feeling of wellbeing. You go out of a morning and it's a lovely, sunny bright day and you're full of life; it's not exactly comedy but it's fun.

I'm a Liverpool supporter but they're going through a bad patch at the moment and a neighbour shouts across to me a few days ago, 'We took all the sick children from Alder Hey hospital to Liverpool's training ground the other day ... just to make the footballers feel better.' That was just on the way to work and I thought that's wonderful, someone there with a sense of humour, having a laugh. And then my mate received a text and it said – 'There's a new dish on the menu to be had at Liverpool's ground ... sour grapes.' And so someone's sitting there with this wonderful gift that they've got from God and the gift is to provide humour.

You get writers like Galton and Simpson and Jimmy Perry, who wrote *Dad's Army*, writing wonderful, wonderful funny things. You see that Captain Mainwaring on the television and it's great, it's uplifting. If you go and see a good comic, it's uplifting, you come out and you feel great, you feel absolutely wonderful.

I know that a good laugh can diffuse a really, really nasty situation because sometimes we do need our spirits uplifted. I was born on 26 September 1939 and the war had started on 3 September. My mam and dad were telling me that they spent lots of time in an air raid shelter. When the German planes used to come over, the sirens would go off and everybody would go to the air raid shelter. People were frightened and depressed. I mean, where they lived wasn't far from the River Mersey, from the docks that got quite a lot of pounding during the war. But I had an aunt, called Doris Brown, and she used to get everyone singing hymns. My mam said the way people's spirits were lifted was absolutely unbeliev-able! They would be singing their heads off in the air raid shelter while the bombs were being dropped. The bombs would be dropping and exploding and they would be singing and lifting their voices. So I think a nice little one liner can defuse the worst of situations and also help to lift people's spirits.

I love making people laugh and I love having a laugh. I think it's a wonderful gift from God. You know the expression 'he laughed till he cried' – I've done that so many times, I have laughed till I've cried. Even now I'm in my seventies and I'm still on the road with Ricky Tomlinson's Laughter Show. It's called 'laughter show' because I think if I can give people something to laugh at, then you know my time on earth hasn't been completely wasted.

RICKY TOMLINSON is an actor and comedian who is well known for his roles in TV and movies, including, *Cracker*, the BAFTA award-winning *The Royle Family*, *Mike Bassett: England Manager* and *Nativity!* Ricky won the National Television Award for most popular comedy performer in 2001.

THEN CAME JESUS

FRANK COTTRELL BOYCE

For thousands of years humans believed that their gods did little else but laugh. On Olympus, in Valhalla, on their Sun Boats, gods were rolling around, clutching their sides all day long, pointing and hooting while we puny mortals messed things up. If by some chance the Mess of the Mortals wasn't messy enough for comedy, the gods could always send a plague of locusts or a quick flood to mess things up a bit more. The thunderbolts of Zeus are the cosmic equivalent of evil children tripping up a blind person for their own amusement. This is the laughter of fear, the laughter that unites one group by expressing contempt for another. There's plenty of it around today in the TV schedules just now, and there's quite a bit of it in the Old Testament – ask Pharaoh.

Then came Jesus. Did Jesus tell jokes? He made a pun – you are Peter and upon this rock – but it was meant to be fond rather than funny. He told stories. The accounts of the parables in the gospels are beautifully spare and pared down. But no one follows anyone up a mountain to hear one paragraph, no matter how beautiful. When he was telling these stories, he must have stretched them out a bit. In the story of the Good Samaritan for instance, his audience would surely have recognised the type of Pharisee who walked by on the other side. Did Jesus use a bit of laughter of recognition to bring him to life? Did he go on a bit about the fancy prayer shawl and the massive phylactery? Did he do his 'priest voice'?

And when the son in the story of the prodigal son spent his inheritance, did the audience mutter 'typical'? Did Jesus lead them on with a hilarious list of stupid ways to blow your money? But having got people to laugh at the stupid son, He then delivered the greatest, most moving twist in the history of storytelling. Hemingway called the return of the prodigal son the most beautiful words ever written down. Here they are:

'... when he was yet a great way off, his father saw him, and had compassion, and ran, and fell on his neck, and kissed him.'

The twist is of course that the prodigal actions are not so much forgiven as totally forgotten. The father has no interest in them whatsoever. All that interests him is that his son is back. What went before barely exists.

'It was meet that we should make merry, and be glad: for this thy brother was dead, and is alive again; and was lost, and is found.'

There's a different kind of laughter here – the big, warm laughter that comes when we are surprised, when the world turns out to be better and bigger than we thought. This is the laugh you laugh when you give someone a present and it's exactly what they wanted but never hoped for. Jesus laughed like this a lot of the time. Think of him suddenly producing vast quantities of excellent wine at the Wedding Feast at Cana. He must have walked home chortling. 'Did you see the look on their faces?' When he fed the five thousand, how did the five thousand feel? Less hungry obviously, but also surprised and impressed. I hope he got a round of applause. Did he nudge St Peter and grin, 'They weren't expecting that, were they?' Did St Peter roll his eyes remembering the unnecessarily massive haul of fish he caught the day they met? Jesus surely laughed that day, standing on the shore, watching that know-it-all fisherman struggle and almost capsize under the sheer weight of divine generosity.

Which brings us to the merriest thing of all – the end of the story, when on Easter morning, after we thought we'd been living through a tragedy, we discover that it's been a comedy all along, that all along there's been a happy ending waiting for us. When St John recounts the story, he even throws in that old comedy standard – the double-take. Mary Magdalene mistakes the risen Lord for a gardener. Yes, God laughs. He laughs with us. He laughs like someone who's bought just the right present on Christmas morning.

And he can't wait to see the look on our faces.

FRANK COTTRELL BOYCE is a screenwriter and children's author, who has penned such famous works as, *Welcome to Sarajevo, The Unforgotten Coat* and *Chitty Chitty Bang Bang Rides Again*. He was the writer of the London Summer Olympics 2012 Opening Ceremony and is the recipient of the Carnegie Medal for children's literature.

I'M STILL STANDING

JO ENRIGHT

So.

Here's the joke I wish I had written.

'What did the zero say to the number eight?'

'I don't know, what did the zero say to the number eight?'

'I like your belt.'

I tell everyone that joke.

It cheers them up.

Even on a very bad day.

In 1991, I 'became' a stand-up comedienne. At about that same time in my life, I also 'became' a Christian. I use the quotation marks for obvious reasons, because with both stand-up comedy and Christianity, you never feel like you have arrived. With both of them, there is always more to learn. You learn the same lessons over and over again. And the majority of the time, even though you're years down the line, you still feel like you're at the very beginning, a novice, a bit of a fraud.

When I first became a Christian, I presumed I would have to give up my 'worldly' pursuit of crafting comedy in front of pub audiences. I worried that it would conflict with my attempt at having a spiritual journey. I worried that by doing comedy I would not be serving God, but rather my ego. I worried about getting addicted to the applause and to the pursuit of fame. I worried about what other Christians would think. I worried because I couldn't get out of the habit of worrying. Phew .... With that amount of anxiety, I needed a laugh more than anyone else I knew.

I decided to give stand-up comedy two years of my life. I'd try it, I thought. Step out. Eat, Pray, Gig ... that sort of thing. During that time, I just happened to meet a group of Christians who were also working in the Arts. I felt relieved. I felt less alone. I felt encouraged. I still do. It's been a hard, lonely, incredible, terrifying, exhilarating and fascinating journey that I am very grateful for. I love the art of comedy. I believe that 'laughter is the shortest distance between two people'. And now, having gigged and prayed (sometimes at the same time) for over two decades, I've started to suspect something about my God. Not only is he with us in our troubles, but, as my Irish forefathers might have said, he's awful great craic.

I try to tell the truth on stage. I am interested in finding jokes about the everyday stuff. I find it helps me reframe difficult experiences and to salvage something from them. I'm not one for waste. I often tell a true story about my Dad's funeral. In Irish families, when someone dies, you often put objects into the coffin with them. In my Dad's coffin, there were many things: whiskey, holy water, holy statues, cigarettes, football trophies, turf, rosary beads, and more. On the day of his funeral, my three sisters, my brother and I all travelled in the funeral car together. As the car crawled along, it was a serious, sombre atmosphere. My eldest sister broke the silence when she quietly remarked on how heavy the coffin was (my Dad was quite a stocky man too). She was very concerned that 'the fellas would be able to carry the weight' she said. Without a moment's thought, she added, 'If that coffin goes over, we'll have an instant Car Boot Sale.' And my sister and I, very quietly, cracked up laughing. Not because we weren't sad, but because that was how we were trying to cope with a very hard time in our lives. I trusted that my Dad, a very witty man, would have loved that punch line. I trusted that sometimes laughter is given to help us get through. To be a healing balm, to comfort our hearts and to dissipate our worries. To give us strength when we have none of our own left.

Sometimes my faith and my work blur into one. When my niece Laura was about four, she asked me a very direct question: 'Auntie Jo, what did God make?' 'Erm …', I said, thinking on my feet … 'He made the clouds … flowers … grass … that sort of thing …' Very deep in thought, she said, 'Mmm … Did he make curtains?' I said, 'No love, factory.' She said, 'Did he make sandals?' 'No love,' I said, 'factory.' 'Did he make cheese?' 'No,' I said, 'factory.' Unimpressed and slightly confused, she pressed me, 'Well … who made God then?' Now I'm not very proud of what I said next. It was ill thought out. I panicked and I said, 'He made himself, love.' She was a smart kid even then. She thought about my answer, walked away, came back ten seconds later and said, 'How did he do his back?' Some material writes itself.

Not so long ago, I did a comedy show at a lovely pub venue in Sheffield. The audience were amazing in that they really let themselves laugh and have fun. As I was leaving the venue, a lady stopped me at the door and said, 'Thank you for your show. You really took my mind off my gas bill!' It's the best review I've ever had. It's going on a poster someday, somewhere. That lady made me laugh and reminded me that when we laugh, we de-stress. For those few minutes, we forget ourselves and our worries and in doing so, sometimes gain new perspective. That's got to be a gift to us from the One who is Love, right?

JO ENRIGHT is a comedian and character actress who has starred and appeared in a number of comedy television and radio programmes including *Lab Rats*, *The Job Lot* and *Life's Too Short*. In 2002 Jo won the Chortle Award for the Best Female Circuit Comic.

DOES GOD WRITE JOKES?

PAUL KERENSA

So, does God have a sense of humour? Well, is the Pope Catholic? Yes. Yes he is. Good, that was easy. Now let's tackle the first, trickier question.

I'm obviously of the opinion that he does. 'Obviously' because I spend much of my time trying to write and perform jokes, so yes, I like to feel that the true originator of these jokes was God. He's my chief writer, if you like. Or I'm just a gag-thief. Whichever way you look at it, God is the Creator, the Originator, the Alpha, the Omega, the set-up, the punch line. Granted, we've been given the free will to use our time on this planet how we wish. I'm sure that not every joke ever uttered is fresh from God's mouth. I certainly have come up with jokes before that I'm convinced are not what God would want from me. Sometimes, we get it wrong. Most of the time, we try to get it right – to publicly speak the words that God puts in our mouths. Every comedian – Christian or not – has at some point stumbled upon some source for humour that does not appear that godly, whether it's a topic like sex, drugs and rock 'n' roll, or a joke at the expense of someone who probably wouldn't appreciate being the butt of the gag.

So this implies that God has a specific sense of humour that may be different to some of our own senses of humour. I'm not going to be so bold as to suggest exactly what God's sense of humour is. Does he prefer slapstick? A pun? Some wry observational comedy? Who knows. I'm sure he does enjoy comedy that changes the world for the better – a satirical comment that gets to the heart of what's wrong with the world. That shows up man's hypocrisy. That makes us laugh and think. But largely, I think it's easier to argue that God's a fan of laughter, rather than pinpointing exactly what style of comedy is his cup of holy tea.

God loves it when we laugh. We are living, breathing, creations of him, by him, and in his own image, and when we experience joy, it is his wish that we make a loud, brash, guffawing sound with our mouths. So I am convinced that a creator God and a creative God has given us this gift for a reason. Laughter bonds us. It lifts us and gets us through the day. It helps us cope, and helps us wrestle with some tricky issues or news events.

So yes, I'm sure it's God-given. Look to the Bible – Isaac was so-named as it means 'He laughs'. And while there is a tendency, especially among non-Christians to see the Bible as far too serious and weighty, bear in mind that when originally written, these were often oral traditions, with biblical stories to be related over campfires. There would be a performative element to some of these stories, and an audience would be enthralled with elements of humour and storytelling throughout. It's the same reason that so many sermons feature and often begin with a funny story or two to engage those listening. If you're laughing, you're listening. So if you were to say that God did in fact not have a sense of humour, does that mean he wouldn't be laughing at these preachers who introduce a sermon with a couple of attempts at humour? Okay, bad example …

PAUL KERENSA is a comedian, writer and author, who is a regular headliner on the comedy circuit and writes for the BBC sitcoms *Miranda* and *Not Going Out*. Paul is also the winner of the ITV1 Take the Mike award.

THE SUDDEN SPATE OF MIRACLES HAD CREATED ITS OWN PROBLEMS FOR LOCAL BUSINESS.

MYCHAILO KAZYBRID

CUTTING-EDGE WIT IN THE BIBLE

ALFIE JOEY

'What you are is God's gift to you, but what you do with yourself is your gift to God.'

US comic Tom Dreesen used this Leo Buscaglia nugget to introduce Frank Sinatra's final performance on 25 February 1995.

If comedic talent is God-given then Laurel and Hardy were bestowed it in abundance, and their response was to use that gift to the hilt; boy did they return a gift to God! More than 75 years after they teamed up to make comedy magic they still make have the ability to make viewers howl. In my case the vintage duo induce shared laughter for me and my two-year-old son! We will watch again and again the way they clown to perfection, inventing, along the way, many of the features we see in today's comedy ... the use of music in comedy, exquisitely timed slapstick, the double take, the look to camera, sight gags, surreal gags, one liners, vaudeville routines ... their influence on the art of being funny is incalculable.

But Stan and Ollie don't just have the gift to make us still laugh out loud. They do something more. Their gift seems to reach out and touch something deep inside, an intangible quality that can make an audience laugh *and* cry! This must be (to this humble scribe least!) the spirituality of humour. There is a science to comedy and hard workers like Bob Monkhouse or Jimmy Carr can manufacture and graft/craft themselves into brilliant comedians but when there is an indisputable ethereal gift at play (L and H, Morecambe and Wise, Tommy Cooper, etc.) it becomes magical, lovable and timeless. Those Comedy Giants use something more than rehearsal, more than training … it stems from pure talent.

Another gift used by many a great clown is self-depreciation, the ability to laugh at oneself. I find it refreshing when churches and faiths do this. As they say, there's no such thing as bad publicity. Dave Allen, Mel Brooks and the Monty Python team all courted controversy because of daring to ridicule elements of religion, but surely they were spoofing, in the main, the people who didn't get it. It seems obvious to me that they were largely lampooning the very same sorts of people Jesus lampooned in the Bible.

This brings me to my favourite piece of Bible wit. It's an account covered by several gospels where the Pharisees and Herodians were trying to trick Jesus into taking a dodgy stand on whether Jews should pay taxes to Rome (Luke 20:20), asking, 'Is it right for us to pay taxes to Caesar or not?'

He saw through their cunning plan and dramatically asked for a coin. 'Show me a denarius. Whose image and inscription are on it?'

'Caesar's,' they replied.

Jesus said to them, 'Then give back to Caesar what is Caesar's, and to God what is God's.' I love the denouement – 'astonished by his answer, they became silent'. Or, as Homer Simpson would've said, 'Doh!'

Jesus was sharp, even cutting edge. Some of his story telling was as exciting as anything delivered by Bill Hicks or Louis C. K. The Good Samaritan has been retold as a parable for kids, but it is ultimately set before a backdrop of sectarian, blood-thirsty hatred. JC wasn't heckled because of these stories, he was put to death because the authorities found his material too subversive. You might say he was crucified because it was the way he told them. And could anyone have mixed comfortably with prostitutes and sinners or have performed unamplified to sizable crowds without some kind of unique humour in his charismatic presence and delivery?

If there is any message here, I suppose it is that there is plenty of humour to be found in scripture stories if you look for it, and faith is more fun (and less po-faced) if you can appreciate the funnies! Oh yes, and if you are giving something up for Lent make sure it's not Laurel and Hardy – they are good for you.

ALFIE JOEY is a comedian and actor, as seen in the BBC sitcoms *Hebburn* and *Ideal*. He is the Breakfast Show presenter on BBC Newcastle.

LAUGHTER IS HOPE

KATIE MULGREW

God.

I don't really remember when I was first taught about God. I think I was, like most children, shown a picture. A picture of an old man with white hair and a long white beard wearing a white robe and brown flip flops. Basically an impossibly cool pensioner who swore by Daz washing powder and most definitely lived in a far warmer climate than my own County of Lancashire.

These were illustrated pictures of God, obviously. Not like, on a night out. The kind you get on social networking sites. Imagine the amount of photos God would be tagged in if he were on Facebook?

Whenever I think about God I never think of him as that snowy-faced man who has clouds for kitchen lino. When I think of God, I think of him as a Dad.

A Dad doing his best.

Not in pristine white cloth but probably a jumper and some jeans from Next. A jeans and jumper combo with toddlers' spit and food dribbled down the front of them. A Dad with a massive jaw and a wide smile.

A Dad who doesn't shout when his kids throw themselves on the floor at the local supermarket. Or knock a glass over when they were told not to run. Or cover the living room wall in felt tips. Or crack a window with a football. A Dad who doesn't shout but laughs.

Even when he's exhausted. Even when he's had a hideous day at work and goes to hang his coat up and not only does the coat rack collapse but pulls half of the hallway wall down with it. He laughs. Loads. At the sheer ruddy ridiculousness of it all.

A Dad who shrugs, smiles and has a giggle. Yeah, real Dads giggle.

I love giggling. I love laughing. It is my absolutely favourite thing to do. I love laughing so much that I have to have a lie down.

I think God is a laugher. He has to be. He's a Dad and Dads are brave.

To me laughter is brave.

Human beings have the most extraordinary gift to use laughter as a survival tool. In my previous job as a teaching assistant in a special needs school I saw tremendous acts of bravery on a daily basis. Families, parents, carers, staff who were stretched and struggling. Caring for severely disabled, violent or damaged children. I never heard complaints. Only laughter.

God is a joker. He has to be. He's a Dad and Dads are jokers.

I've seen friends joke in spite of their circumstances. Friends who have suffered heartbreak. Friends who have suffered enormous loss. They've joked and laughed in the face of it.

How brilliant is that? To laugh right in Death's big stupid face.

To me laughter is hope.

It is the most visual and audible expression of hope that any human can express. When I feel like the world is an irreparable place and we are irreparable people, seeing someone or hearing someone laugh makes me feel instantly hopeful.

To me laughter is love.

So God *is* a LOL-er. He has to be.

KATIE MULGREW is a stand-up comedian and lover of chicken kievs.

JOY GIVER

JIMMY CRICKET

In that great classic inspirational song 'I Believe', there's a line that goes …

> 'Every time I hear a baby cry,
> Or touch a leaf,
> Or see the sky,
> Then I know why I believe.'

Now close the door and don't tell anybody. But when I sing that song to myself (usually in the bath), I add an extra line that goes:

> 'Every time I look out into a crowd,
> And hear them laugh out loud,
> It makes me oh so proud,
> Then I know why I believe.'

Laughter has such healing power. It has to come from our Creator. I've lost count of the number of times I've heard people say they've been through a worrying time in their lives, but a couple of hours in a live comedy show was just the tonic they needed. The release of pent-up emotion. The clearing away of cobwebs. They come out reinvigorated and refreshed, ready to take on the world again.

What was it Jesus said, 'When two or more are gathered, I am there.' Of course he meant that we get together in prayer and acknowledge him as our Saviour who died for our sins. And that in itself will over flow our hearts with joy. When we go into the world to spread the word, we're also spreading love, peace and, yes, laughter.

What preacher worth his salt doesn't add a touch of humour to his sermons, and when he gets it right you can hear the laughter ring out just like the steeple bells. Far from detracting from his message, it's enhanced and embellished it. Some of the loudest laughter I've ever heard has been in places of worship. That and the singing of some of the most beautiful songs of worship, and don't you come out feeling such a glow.

I'm often asked in radio interviews, did Christ laugh and joke? Well, yes! If I'd been a fly on the wall in Biblical times, I'm sure walking along the road with his disciples I would have seen a less serious side. Then there were the great miracles. After he'd grubbed up the faithful with the loaves and fishes, I'm sure they were ready for a bit of fun. Any comic who has done a cabaret after the audience have had a four course meal knows how contented and receptive they can be.

Then there is the chap he raised from the dead. They could have been having a meal afterwards and JC leaned across and said, 'Come on, Lazarus, get a life.' Well maybe not.

I'm sure our Lord indulged in humour. You just have to

fill in the blanks in between the times he was preparing for and eventually saving mankind.

When we get on with God by leading good lives, he shines through our whole personality, and when we get a good laugh from innocent wholesome humour, well, it is like music; when it is really good you just know that it comes from above.

I think it was the great poet and philosopher Ralph Waldo Emerson who said, 'Nature laughs through flowers.' I think God laughs through human beings and when we share a laugh, we're sharing our love for one another and his love for us.

I'm sure he laughs in his own way at me. Especially when I'm in the bath making up my own words to 'I Believe'.

JIMMY CRICKET is an Irish comedian who starred in his own TV show, *And There's More*, and the radio series, *Jimmy's Cricket Team,* which was written by the late Eddie Braben. Recently he has been guesting on John Bishop's *Only Joking*.

GOD MAKES THINGS SILLY

SHERRIE HEWSON

Well one would hope God has a sense of humour. I would think that everybody has to have a sense of humour to actually even live in this world. So God has a sense of humour in the sense of he makes things funny, silly, ridiculous, impossible – life I mean. And so if you're able to laugh at that then you'll get through whatever, that's how I think of it; just stop and laugh! Humour is what life is all about.

Because life is very silly, and we all have very silly, difficult moments in our lives, and if you can smile as soon as you get out of bed in the morning your day will be okay. If you get up and you're grumpy – and we all are sometimes – if you can smile, that smile will bring your day to you. If you get up and you refuse to smile and you get angry you will be angry for the rest of the day.

So I think humour is in everything really, everything. The world is so beautiful you've only got to look at a flower or a bird to think 'What?!! That's impossible' … and that beauty and humour, that's all you need in life. I'm not saying we all can all the time, that would be a perfect situation, but I feel if we could find that in ourselves, that humour and beauty, then we'd all be really nice people wouldn't we?

Animals make me laugh as well. Baboons make me laugh – if you look at a baboon's bottom you could say it's the ugliest thing in the world, but it makes us laugh, so it's not ugly. I'm a great animal lover and one of my favourites is the orang-utan, and if you watch orang-utans they have great beauty and such humour.

Oh yes, I do think there is laughter in heaven, and I think there's great laughter. God would have been chuckling in my life many times, and that's what's kept me sane. I've had dreadful times, really, really, really, bad times when I have dropped to my knees and said 'God if you are there do something about this!' and it has always worked, strangely, and I suppose it's because I believe. But I've had silly times, funny times you know when I've fallen off stage, because I'm very clumsy; there have been so many funny times in my life.

I remember my granddad died and we had the funeral and the cars turned up and he was in the front hearse, obviously, and then the three black cars behind him. My mum had a big Afghan Hound, I had an enormous Weimaraner, we had another two poodles, and unfortunately, all at the same time, they all got out and started running down the road. So everybody then had to get out of the hearse, everybody in their black clothes, running down the road after these blooming dogs! And there's granddad at the front and we're all saying to the driver 'No don't go, wait! Wait! We're not behind you, we're not behind you!' It was like the Keystone Cops. Somebody ran to the front and went and banged on the front of the hearse and said 'Stop! Stop!', and the driver asked, 'What?' 'The dogs! The dogs!' Everybody got muddy, we had to grab the dogs, get them back in … oh it was funny. We couldn't stop laughing; so there have been many times like that.

People say I do bring happiness and that is very humbling. If that's something I've done in my life before I go then I'm very proud of that. I think it's the most precious gift to have to make people laugh.

And I think if God taught anybody anything that's the one thing – always have humour in your life and you can get through everything.

SHERRIE HEWSON is a comedy actress and presenter, co-hosting *Loose Women* and featuring in numerous TV shows and dramas, most notably *Coronation Street* and *Benidorm*.

LAUGHABLE SUGGESTION

MILTON JONES

No, God doesn't have a sense of humour! How dare you. Of course he doesn't. God just likes beards, the smell of church halls, and old ladies wearing hats. Everyone knows this.

Okay, the Bible does say that men and women are made in God's image – you know, that we're all a bit like him. But we all know that God is like a weak old man, so we should all be like that too. I know I am. God is not approachable. He told me – well, that's the impression I got, from a distance.

Monkeys are a problem! All that pointless mucking about. Bananas are largely unhelpful as well. I mean the vitamins are useful, but all that look-at-me yellow and their ridiculous shape were a big mistake. Then if you accidentally step on a skin, or combine monkeys and bananas – well I don't even want to think about it! I'm sure if they were being created again the Almighty would do it all quite differently. Monkeys would be well behaved and bananas grey, square and made safely out of Velcro.

The problem as I see it is that laughing is a communal activity, and it tends to bring people together. God doesn't like that, I'm guessing. If he did he would be a different sort of god. More friendly. No, I don't think about it.

Someone breaking wind at a funeral — that can be awkward too. Best to think about something else. Pinch yourself. Take a deep breath. Okay, maybe not that last one.

You see, expressing elation in the form of abstract roars and sniffles is surely a sign of weakness, and trust me — with these hiccups of the soul, prevention is better than cure. If anything looks as if it's getting out of order, or things are about to get a bit intense just withdraw to a private room, or put on your headphones and listen to that track again, the one that goes 'la la la la la'.

I mean some people say that laughter is what fills the gap between what we'd like to happen and the realities of life. But I believe these moments should be completely ignored. To do otherwise would be to admit we don't know what's going on. To laugh along with everyone else merely unites us in a moment of helplessness. If you enjoy a misunderstanding, that's a sure sign that your life is on the slide. (The slide to depravity, not a slide in a park, obviously. Sorry, I'm not helping.)

When I get to heaven, as I'm sure I will, there will be no laughing — just the occasional song, and maybe a bit of nodding from a distance. Looking forward to it.

The good news is that if you continually resist the temptation to feel these emotions, they eventually go away. And an added bonus of losing the ability to laugh is that you'll probably lose the ability to cry as well, and that will save you any number of awkward situations. Yes, then you won't be able to actively empathize with people in their suffering. Then you can just shake your head from a distance and silently get on with your own specially padded private life. Good eh? What's more you can entertain yourself by telling other people what *they* should be doing. Yes, just put all that hidden anger into bossing people about.

Occasionally I have the odd passing thought that God might not be like a weak old man, perhaps more like an angry teenager or a mischievous Dad trying out jokes on his kids – and we just don't get them. Or that perhaps this is just stage one – and it's all part of something much bigger. But clearly that can't possibly be the case because then we'd have to re-think everything. Then we'd be more like babies trying to understand a motorcar, only able to react by making random gurgles and noises.

But I think only children should enjoy laughing. Their emotions have yet to evolve the tenacity to run for years in sub-zero temperatures. Children like splashing in puddles for goodness sake! In fact I always think that one good measure of how mature you are is how little fun you are for children. If they like you, that's probably because you're like them! And they're vulnerable – and no one wants to be that. Thinking about it, almost any interaction with another human being is regrettable isn't it? That's rhetorical by the way.

The other truly terrible thought I have occasionally is that it's all the other way round. You know, that softness might be a strength. But we won't dwell on that. Whoops, I almost felt something there. Like a bit of sick coming into your mouth at the wrong moment.

What if someone could prove to me that God isn't like a weak old man and that he's really quite different? How would I feel then? Well, obviously, I'd feel nothing.

MILTON JONES is a comedian, writer and author who appears regularly on *Mock the Week* and has starred in *Live at the Apollo* and *Michael McIntyre's Comedy Roadshow*. His acclaimed Radio 4 show has won a Silver Sony Award.

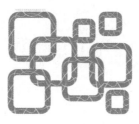

Life is not about waiting for the storms to pass … it's about learning to dance in the rain.

Vivian Greene

A good laugh is a sign of love; it may be said to give us a glimpse of, or a first lesson in, the love that God bears for every one of us.

Karl Rahner

As the bridegroom rejoices in his bride, so will your God rejoice in you.

Isaiah 62:5

THE EDITOR REFLECTS

Father James Martin, an American Jesuit, talks about how someone might have fallen into the trap of becoming a gloomy Christian. He reflects on how a lot of our art, paintings, sculptures can depict Jesus, Mary, the apostles, etc. as being a little serious, all gloomy looking. How many images have you seen of Jesus after his resurrection smiling?[1] I mean come on … you've just saved humankind and sealed the deal for eternal life – even Elvis and Frank Sinatra were smiling at their comeback gigs!

Scripture tells us that Jesus is the Alpha and Omega, the beginning and the end (Revelation 22:13), through whom God the Father made all things (Colossians 1:16). Well if he is, then he must be the first and last in also having a sense of humour!

According to the Old Testament prophet Zephaniah, God sings and dances out of joy for us all (Zephaniah 3:17). God is more than capable of radiating joy, as, similarly in Luke 21:10, it tells us that Jesus was 'filled with joy by the Holy Spirit'. The actual word used for joy is *agalliao* a Greek word that means 'rejoiced greatly; to leap and skip for joy; rejoicing to the fullest extent'. People ask, if Jesus was on earth today what would he

1. James Martin, talk given at REC 2011.

be doing … well in accordance with that, he might be having a dance-off with Beyoncé! Just throwing it out there … if he's the beginning and the end, at least put his name down for a moonwalk! But that word *agalliao*, appears eleven times in the New Testament, that is some serious celebrating. Even at the Saviour's birth we are told about an incident that happened a few fields away when angels appeared to shepherds in order to announce this birth: 'I bring you news of great joy, a joy to be shared by the whole world'. Now surely you're going to have to come up with a few funnies during your life with an intro like that! All right there's no *Live at the Apollo* smoke, but that was one of the main reasons he came into the world – to bring more joy into it! (Could the same argument be used for the vocation of a comedian?)

I do think that Jesus presented a lot of funny situations in his life, poking fun at hypocrites who do good works to have them trumpeted before them, 'having a plank in your eye', 'a camel going through the eye of a needle', etc. Might he have been even funnier? Well, it's not always easy to remember one-liners a week after seeing a comic let alone thirty years down the line (which is when many people believe the first gospel was written). Also, would God in his providence have allowed one-liners to go into the gospels? When you think about it, these are stories and events we reflect on and hear over and over again, and would it really work for a priest or vicar to be standing up on a Sunday morning reading out familiar jokes from the gospels, and you get a guy at the back heckling, 'Heard it, tell us one we don't know!' To be honest I have to stop myself from time to time from slipping into old habits, wrapping up a homily and saying 'You've been a great crowd and I've been Father Frankie Mulgrew.'

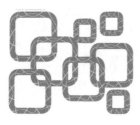

Comedians and clowns are likely to have a high place in heaven because they must be near to the heart of God.

Thomas Merton

What would happen if we hid what little sense of humour we had? Let each of us humbly use this to cheer others.

St Teresa of Avila

I have told you this so that my own joy may be in you and your joy be complete.

John 15:11

LOL MOMENTS IN GLORY

TOM ELLIOTT

So, having been asked the question, 'Does God LOL?', I can confirm that yes he does. I have just checked. The book of life does in fact have 'LOL' written in red sharpie pen on every page. Though, this is all pretty obvious, after all, he sees every little action, thought, word and error of human existence. I've recently thought that observing human life must be similar to the battery of a man's shaver dying half way around the face. Awkward, infuriating, but hilarious.

Of course, there are three particular occasions when God might ROTFWL (roll on the floor with laughter), or in his case, perhaps ROTCWL (roll on the clouds with laughter). This extreme outburst of holy chortle happens on a regular basis.

I wouldn't mind betting that when building the ark, Noah had a few good LOL moments with God. If Noah existed these days, I'm sure his sense of humour would have played a part in this story.

Noah would have purchased a clothed, child-sized, mannequin, which he would freeze over so it's contained in a block of ice. Then he would have stood in front of the ark shouting 'Look what has happened to little Harry!' and giggle at the reactions of people around.

Of course, the 'LOL moments in Glory' continue when the young angels complain that 'Hide and Seek' is no fun with an omniscient creator.

Of course, God's laughter comes from a place of love for his people. After all, he surely made us with all our quirks for his own entertainment? Heaven's comical entertainment is far more than *Hymn Factor* or *Strictly Come Tithing*. I reckon God's got us on Channel Earth repeat. If he misses a regular show due to new heavenly arrivals, he can catch up on it later when the Angel Gabriel has left him alone.

Whilst God might 'LOL' at us, I believe he may also be a joker himself. When someone turns up to heaven, he opens the gate a little and says, 'Not until you've shown some sort of identification!'

So, in my opinion, God does indeed LOL. In fact, he ROTFWL.

TOM ELLIOTT is a comedian, magician and Christian communicator from Gloucestershire. He performs across the UK, writes a weekly blog and is an ambassador for Compassion UK.

DOES GOD LOL?

JO BRAND

Does God, or your affiliate God, LOL?

Does he/she 'laugh out loud' or does he/she have/ send 'lots of love'? (I may refer to Lord Leveson for his ruling on that one.)

Yes, I reckon the God I'm thinking about enjoys a good old belly laugh, a giggle or a hoot at appropriate moments. It's a wonder what, from his bejewelled seat in the highest heavens, he finds to double up about some-times. Maybe he sees the funny side?

I give you a brief example from one of his authorised books:

Abraham was ambling about the campsite one day and shouted to Sarah to make some cakes because they had visitors, and it wasn't the painters. These people happened to ask where Sarah was and he said: 'In the tent.'

One of these blokes said: 'About this time next year I shall come back, and your wife Sarah will have a son.'

Sarah, from inside the tent, *laughed*. 'At my time of life? My husband is old!' (Euphemistically put, of course, and in the best possible taste for the Bible.)

Abraham was a little perplexed too because he wasn't sure he was up to the job either. He was wondering what

Sarah was *laughing* about and overheard her own slight misgivings since she had been dealing with hot flushes for months, if not years!

At this point God stepped in and seemed to suggest that just about anything is possible. Abraham then took the moral high ground with Sarah, forcing her to lie and deny that she had *laughed*. But old Abraham replied rather archly: 'Yes, you did *laugh*.'

I guess that's why we have St Sarah, Saint of Laughter. I know what isn't funny though, and I think God's with me on this one, and that's being hungry. Being hungry and seeing no future, not even knowing what a future is apart from having to get through the next day. Laughter is a luxury in those circumstances.

And, summarising from 'A Collection of Wise Sayings' (The Book of Proverbs): 'He who is generous to the poor, lends to the Lord, who will recompense him for his deed.'

JO BRAND is a BAFTA award-winning comedian, writer and actress who has starred in her own television programmes, and who appears regularly on *Have I Got News For You*, *QI* and *Splash!*.

EVERYBODY LAUGHS

MICK MILLER

When I was asked to contribute to this book, I had to think about the question, 'Does God LOL?' The answer is obvious, he must do! I mean, someone who creates an aardvark and makes us spell it like that must have been having a laugh.

Millions of people across the world have faith and I believe that God must *laugh out loud because* every single one of those people, whether they are rich or poor, do exactly that – *laugh!* I'm sure that many of the contributors to this book will have said the same thing, laughing is very good for you. We all feel much better after a good belly laugh. Laughing is a God-given gift to us all, and if it isn't, why did he create Ken Dodd and Peter Kay?

So, in an effort to make you laugh out loud, I have decided to tell you a little story. I hope you (and God) find it funny.

One day, a man was in his garden when there was a huge thunderclap and a bolt of lightning. As he stood there, he heard a voice saying, 'Keith, this is God. I want you to do something for me.' The man stood there looking perplexed and said, 'Who did you say you are?' 'God!' came the reply. The man was puzzled as the voice went on to say, 'The weather is going to change, there is going to be low pressure with a cold front on the way. This coupled with the jet stream is going to cause torrential rain and flooding, so I want you to build a boat.' Keith replied, 'A boat?' 'Yes,' said God, 'A blooming big one.' Keith asked for a bit more information and God went on to explain that the boat needed to have eight floors and that each floor should be fitted with fish tanks. Keith didn't understand, so he asked God to repeat the instructions. God told him again and was most specific about the eight floors filled with fish tanks. 'What should I do with the fish tanks?' asked Keith. God went on to explain that the rain was going to cause serious flooding and that he was most concerned about the fish that were being sold at the nearby garden and fish pond centre. He told Keith to go and get breeding pairs of every type of carp that they had. 'I need you to fill all of the tanks with Koi Carp, Ghost Carp, Silver Carp, Common Carp, Crucian Carp, Mud Carp and every other type of carp that you can get hold of. I really love carp.' Again, Keith questioned the instructions and mentioned that the centre was noted for the huge amounts of different types of Carp that they stocked. Again, God explained that he really liked carp, and didn't want them to get wiped out in the flood that was due. He insisted that Keith filled all the tanks on all eight floors with breeding pairs of carp, which would save his favourite type of fish from extinction.

It was at this point that Keith suddenly understood what God wanted, 'I get it now,' he said, 'You want me to build a MULTI-STOREY CARP ARK!'

MICK MILLER, who affectionately refers to himself as 'The Bald Guy with the Long Hair', was a regular on TV's *The Comedians*. Recent notoriety has seen him playing Johhny Vegas's dad in *Ideal* and appearing in the Royal Variety Performance

GOD CREATED THE HEAVENS AND THE MIRTH

TONY VINO

Picture the scene, Heaven. Jesus is on the phone to his buddy Saint Peter.

'Yo, Pete, gather the crew it's party time at my place.'

'You sure J-bomb, that's a lot of people.'

'It will be fine, plenty of space, remember my Father's house has many rooms.'

'So who should we invite? John?'

'Yeah, I love that guy.'

'You reckon Thomas will come?'

'Doubt it.'

'Should we get some nibbles?'

'Absolutely, I'll buy some roquefort, gruyere and smoked cheddar.'

'Urgh, no way!'

'What have I told you before about denying cheeses?'

'You want me to bring the booze?'

'Its cool, bro, I've got a couple of cisterns of water in the back … leave it with me.'

'You legend. I'll bring some Blue Nun. Seriously

though, is it cool with your Father – there's gonna be a lot of noise and a lot of crazy shenanigans.'

'Mate, he'll be there, it is a laugh after all.'

'Okay, I'll make some calls.'

'Petey Boy, you're a rock. Oh and by the way, the doorbell is broken so just keep knocking and I will answer.'

Does God have a sense of humour? Of course he does, he invented it. No one ever questioned whether Alexander Graham Bell would have agreed with Bob Hoskins' assertion 'It's good to talk'. God also invented things that are inherently funny like puppies and farts.

I believe the nature of God is best revealed in the person of Christ.

'So tell me what Jesus was like.'

I thought you'd never ask.

Jesus was a radical non-violent subversive who hung around with a load of travelling hippies, made parties better, did miracles, mixed with prostitutes and the socially unacceptable. He opposed the humourless empire, spoke using profound parables, was totally unpredictable, totally loving and totally forgiving. Heaven sent him, religious leaders couldn't stand him, children couldn't get enough of him, the world couldn't accept him, the grave couldn't keep him and the future belongs to him.

He sounds a bit dull, huh …

Most people who love God would agree he is full of joy, life, laughter and fun. However these can often be lacking in many peoples experience of church and Christianity. So there can be a disconnect between our perception of God and our experience of religion. This makes a lot of sense. God is the source of light and when we try to seal that light in a box, it ain't half dark inside. This does beg the question of why I think we can do such a woefully bad job of representing God when we supposedly gather in his name – that's for another book (the Bible). Suffice to say if we are looking to follow Jesus we need to be people of good humour. Some people light up the room when they enter it, others when they leave it. In fact I reckon lack of humour should be the eighth deadly sin, along with talking loudly on trains. In James 4:6 it says 'God opposes the proud'. If we take ourselves too seriously we are incapable of seeing the funny side of things, including puppies and farts.

What is not funny is the idea that we are a mere clump of atoms attached to a rock spinning around a random universe without any innate worth, value or purpose. This paradigm leaves concepts such as love and beauty mere biological impulses bereft of any sublime quality. God is reduced to a concept and life has no point. Denying the existence of the one who made existence possible is the one thing I imagine doesn't make God laugh out loud.

TONY VINO is a top pro comedian who straddles the worlds of comedy clubs, corporate entertainment, churches and festivals. He co-hosts a popular weekly men's podcast with Alex Willmott, available on iTunes.

LAUGHTER HEALS

BOBBY BALL

I think God has got a sense of humour, yeah ... he made me and he made the wife so he certainly has got a sense of humour.

Yes, God does want us to be happy and to laugh. I'll tell you for why – laughter belongs to God and everything other than joy, is not of God I believe. Because to have God within you, you can only be full of joy! And I'll tell you something else and everybody must try this; you can't laugh and worry at the same time. Because the minute you start to laugh your worries are gone. And I believe that's how God wants us to be – so joyful. And we should be, because God said we're living forever, so what's not to be joyful about? Look at me I'm going to live forever, not only that but I'm only 26 ... because that's when my life started, when I found Jesus.

There's a funny side to a conversion. There's a friend of mine (he's Welsh), he became converted and somebody said 'Wow! Miracles happen, he's speaking in tongues.' My friend said, 'I wasn't, I was speaking in Gaelic.'

I'll tell you what was funny about my conversion: when I found Jesus I was crying, but they were tears of joy. Outside I was really crying but inside I was laughing ... I was over the moon, it was unbelievable! When I first found Jesus, I was driving along and I was crying, and I got to the traffic lights and I looked at a bloke in the car opposite me. He looked at me and said, 'You all right, what's up?' He thought I was crying but I was full of joy! I think there would have been joy, a real joy about Jesus's miracles happening.

God sees the funny side of our situations. I said to my wife Yvonne when I first found Jesus, I said 'Erm ... I think I'll go to Bible College and be a pastor.' She said, 'I'm leaving you.' I said 'Why?' 'I'm not being a pastor's wife', she said. I said 'I'll be an evangelist.' She said, 'Okay, that'll do.'

I do think Jesus would have been funny and had a laugh; I would have loved to have been with him, because I think he would have been a good-time fella. This is what fascinates me: I used to be a welder so I worked with a lot of men. There were twelve disciples, and amongst those twelve disciples there would have been a comic; there would have been the funny one. Find out who it is and I'll give you a pound!

Laughter heals, it's been proven. Scientists have proved that laughter heals, because it sets these endorphins (the body's natural feel-good chemicals) off in your body, so laughter heals. Laughter is a healing process that's why I think laughter is God's tool. He tells us continually not to worry, trust in me, don't have problems, give them all to me. Why? So we can laugh and enjoy life!

BOBBY BALL is one half of the duo Cannon and Ball, who held the comedy prime time TV family slot in the 1980s, and who have gone on to discover new audiences over the years through recent appearances on popular comedy, drama and reality TV shows.

This isn't laugh out funny but I remember one time being in church and seeing a family with a very sweet baby.

(I've drawn bunnies instead of people).

In the pew behind was a small child who also noticed the adorable baby.

It tickled me to see the boy recognising the sweetness of the baby yet being unaware at how adorable and lovely he was.

I felt God having a laugh to himself. He gently pointed out that I'm also unaware of how adorable and lovely I am to Him...

SIMONE LIA

THE EDITOR'S THOUGHTS

Woody Allen once said 'When you do comedy you are not sitting at the grown-ups table.' Around 2000 years before this quote there was a sound bite from a divine carpenter from Galilee advising people that unless we become like little children we won't get into the kingdom of heaven (Matthew 18:3). The two quotes aren't too dissimilar. I know, maybe they knew the same rabbi? But that's what a comedian is: someone who for 20, 30, 50 minutes loses their inhibitions, becomes childlike in order to be free and open to explore and gag about whatever.

Children have many attributes, but for the sake of this argument let's highlight a few. For example a child is innocent, full of fun and mischievous – like the story I heard about the six-year-old girl who wanted a hamster for Christmas but figured she would get it if she started out by asking her parents for a horse! And that's what a comedian is invited to be – childlike – and what an audience is invited to be, in order to 'enter' and 'go with' the comedian's world of lunacy and ideas of fun. It doesn't just work for comedy. I heard a famous football player being interviewed about his great ability, and he simply put it down to the fact that he was like a child when he stepped onto the pitch. So it's not only comedy that encourages one to become childlike; but that's for another book.

Studies reckon that children laugh on average between 300 – 400 times a day, while adults average around 15 times. I find that hard to believe … as many as 15 times? You gotta meet my bank manager. But we adults have got some catching up to do. And we complain about sitcom re-runs? By this assessment, could an argument be created for Jesus inviting us to laugh our way into heaven?

I went out to Kenya to work on the missions a few years back and there was one experience in particular that has always stayed with me. I was invited to a prayer group that was being led by street children who were being re-habilitated. There was a group of kids aged from six to fourteen in a packed room. When the prayer service began, I was overwhelmed by the authentic love and tangible faith these young people had as they sang God's praises. Yet I sat there knowing that these children had had everything taken from them, and even the people they had trusted the most in their lives had abused or abandoned them. Yet through their childlike faith they had a joy that was so real, so tangible, that it gave me a master class in what it really is to have faith in God. Their joy, I believe, came from childlike trust that God is in control of all things.

The American author Mark Twain wrote once about what he thought led to a happy life and as you'll see they are all qualities that little children excel in:

'Sing like no one's listening,
Love like you've never been hurt,
Dance like nobody's watching,
And live like its heaven on earth.'

RELIGION DOESN'T HAVE TO BE DULL

DON MACLEAN

During my many years of presenting *Good Morning Sunday* on BBC Radio 2 I had many daft emails from listeners who had had a sense of humour bypass. It was 5 November and I happened to say, 'Well tonight's bonfire night when we go out and set fire to Roman candles. I shall stay in; it'd be just my luck to bump into a dyslexic protestant.' Not that funny but surely recognisable as 'a joke'. Within three minutes my producer had received an email that said, 'It's people like that Don Maclean that are perpetrating the sectarian violence in Northern Ireland.'

For many years I've campaigned against 'po-faced Christianity'; nothing does Christians more harm. You know what I'm talking about; people who find it impossible to mix humour and religion. How do they cope when something funny happens in church as it often does, usually during the readings?

A rather nervous chap once approached the microphone. 'The first reading is from the prophet Isaiah', he began. During the reading he had to say three times the phrase 'camels in throngs' and each time he said 'camels in thongs'. Let's be honest, a person looks funny enough in a thong let alone a camel! We collapsed in hysterics.

There are many words in Genesis lying in wait for the unsuspecting reader. You will recall a tribe called the Hittites who crop up at regular intervals. The reading was from Genesis 27. The reader spoke with great confidence: 'Rebekah said to Isaac, "my life will not be worth living if Jacob takes unto wife one of these high titty women"'.

Every parish has a reader who really fancies themselves and for some reason they're usually Welsh. Why is that? Probably because the Welsh don't really care whether you're listening to them or not because they are listening to themselves. Think of all the great Welsh orators: Richard Burton, Dylan Thomas, Anthony Hopkins, as they speak they are hanging on their every syllable as it comes back to them and they are thinking 'my word but that sounds magnificent'. We have such a reader at my church; he's Welsh and he's retired, and because he's retired he has the time, when it's his turn to read, to learn the readings so that instead of looking at the book, he is able to stare at the congregation and declaim. The congregation are desperate for him to make a mistake but he never has until a few weeks ago. He stood at the lectern glanced down at the book then, from memory, recited the first reading beautifully while we all sat there in grudging admiration. He then glanced at the book again, fixed us with a fervent gaze and declared 'the second reading is from St Paul's epistle to the Fallopians'. As one, the entire congregation said, 'Yes! Thank you, Lord!'

The clergy is not immune from faux pas. We have a permanent deacon, a devout man who delights in reading the gospel. There was a certain fervour in his eyes as he launched into the feeding of the 5000 from the Gospel of St John: 'when they had all had enough to eat, they gathered up the scraps and there was enough left over to fill twelve hamsters.' Not very much when you think about it.

'The Wedding Feast' is a favourite of mine since Sunday School days. Having read this particular gospel, our priest decided to elaborate on it in his sermon. You will recall that there are five wise bridesmaids and they have oil in their lamps and more oil in jars. When the bridegroom arrives however the five foolish bridesmaids have no oil in their lamps. I never expected the priest to say it, but he did: 'Tell me honestly, would you rather be in the light with the wise virgins or in the dark with the foolish ones?' No contest really!

Religion doesn't have to be dull and humourless to be effective any more than medicine has to taste terrible in order to do you good. Pass it on!

DON MACLEAN is a comedian and presenter who hosted BBC Radio 2's popular *Good Morning Sunday* for more than 15 years. Don is also known for starring in *Crackerjack* and appearing in pantomime up and down the land. He was awarded a Papal Knighthood in 2012.

GOD WANTS ME TO HAVE FUN!

JUDY MCDONALD

Does God have a sense of humour?

Definitely. I mean sticking animals and a dude on a boat for a while (Genesis 5:32–10:1) ... that's funny. You know that set the precedent for some of these cruise lines who have been having problems of late. You think it is bad to have no turn-down service or running water for a few days?

Really I think God is into physical comedy, the ultimate sight gag was Abraham bringing his son to the altar saying 'I'm gonna kill him', and God's like, 'Just kidding never mind ... don't do it, thanks for listening to me, that was very impressive!' How do you think future camping trips went for that father and son?

And sending the Three Wise Men on a chase after a star; not only were they men, they were wise men! Yet they can't get it together to ask for directions (Matthew 2:1–2)?

I think he does laugh out loud, even though he's all knowing and full of love and all that good stuff and has a very long white beard. I think God's humour is the purest form of humour, because it is joy. Like when a parent looks at their kid and chuckles as the child works on a project and isn't making a good job of it. The parent doesn't laugh because they are messing up, but because the child is, well, *their* child and their heart swells with joy just watching them. God looks at us with just that joy! Pure joy. I think the best humour down here on earth is filled with that same joy.

Sometimes, according to my older sisters when I was growing up, he looks at us when we are being bad and cries. That's when it's storm season.

It's allowable to laugh and be funny all while loving God.

Sometimes I think people feel like 'if you're funny you're not serious about God'. I think that's so sad, John XXIII was a great, funny Pope. He was once asked 'How many people work in the Vatican?' and he said 'About half.' That's a good joke! Would you argue that he was not holy because he told jokes? Of course not.

I think a lot of people think maybe God doesn't have a sense of humour, or that he would not enjoy what we find funny. I think those kinds of people who don't think God gets our jokes, really don't appreciate how *big* and immense God is. Maybe they keep God up on the shelf and take him down for Mass, or when they need to do well on an exam at school and then put him back on the shelf when it's time to have 'fun'.

Jesus knew God … like Jesus and God were pretty tight. I don't know if you know your church history like I do? But God didn't just call Jesus 'Hey Jesus,' he was 'His son' and when Jesus refers to God its 'Abba', it's

'Father', it's 'Daddy' and that's the kind of relationship I really want to strive for and where I really think that God is calling us into having that kind of intimate, close relationship. Me and my dad joke around a lot. Why do I think my Heavenly Father can't have fun as well?

Anyone who has worked for a Church sees signs all the time of God's humour…for instance I don't know if you've ever experienced this, but I've worked for several different parishes … it's almost like a United Nations meeting, the screaming and the hair pulling, that goes on over what type of banner to put up for the fish fry. Or where the flowers should be placed in the hall for the altar and rosary society luncheon? It's a wonder the Church has lasted as long as it has. But that's if it was up to people.

I think the Church in itself isn't really laugh out loud funny, but I think its people, the humans who run it are. Because they are just that, human. I think humans are funny by God's design. He knows how humans act and he still trusts them to spread his word and carry on his church. As any good parent knows, a sense of humour is essential when dealing with 'your creation', and again, why would God be any different?

I think what God does do is gives us the free will that allows us to see things from his perspective. To see things like 'you know what, I just lost my job … but when I really think about it I hated that job', and to be open to what God has in store for us, I think is great. I think it's not laughing at us, but with us, if we can take the time to stop and laugh and say 'Oh my gosh, what just happened!' Thank you, Jesus that as I look back in my life, that some things I really thought I wanted, would have been horrible for me! Losing my last job opened me up to being a professional Catholic comedian. Now you have to admit that is pretty funny.

I don't think God gave us this life just to be miserable. My God at least is not a task master. He's not up there ticking off his piece of paper when I do something bad. He's rooting for me and he wants me to enjoy this life. He wants me to have fun, he wants me to experience the fullness of life, and he's laughing with me when I'm laughing and crying with me when I'm crying. He's on my side … and he wants us to laugh out loud!

JUDY MCDONALD is an American comedian who spends her time traveling around the US and beyond playing Catholic parishes, universities, conferences, military bases and comedy clubs.

IMPOSSIBLY FUNNY – HUMOUR IN THE MIRACLES

JOHN ARCHER

'Nobody expects the Spanish Inquisition!' So said the *Monty Python* team, and it's true. I'm not expecting it, I don't know anyone who is, but that's not the point; the point is that surprise is a key element in comedy and Monty Python knew that. Some would say surprise is the first rule of comedy, and of course it is a key element in the craft of magic too. As a side note, when I say 'magic' I mean conjuring, trickery, sleight of hand, not the mysterious dark arts. Please don't burn me, I just cheat for fun. As a comedy magician my job is to try to create magical and comedic surprises, and one thing I have noticed is that they often elicit the same response: laughter. When something happens that we're not expecting we often laugh. The bible is full of amazing and unexpected things, miracles that defy explanation, some make me laugh just reading them, others must have made biblical dwellers chuckle with surprise at least.

The Old Testament takes some wonderful twists and turns. I particularly love the story of Balaam and his donkey (Numbers 22: 21–39). God certainly has a soft spot for donkeys; Jesus himself was happy to ride into town on one. They are friendly unassuming beasts, at worst stubborn, but I'm sure I'm not the only one who sees them on the humorous side of the animal kingdom. So I think even Balaam's servants must have seen the funny side when Balaam's own donkey started misbehaving. It runs off into a field, then crushes Balaam's foot against the rock, and then, to add insult to injury, it lays down while he is still astride it. That would be enough to have me falling off my donkey with laughter, but it gets better, much better. I like to imagine the next bit playing out a little like a scene from *Shrek*, with the donkey's voice masterfully played by a cool Eddie Murphy. The donkey speaks to him in a very matter of fact way: 'Hey what have I done?' Now I am assuming that Balaam's donkey hasn't spoken to him before, perhaps he is a little shocked but he just goes ahead and replies, 'You've made me look like an idiot'. Erm … Earth to Balaam, who's the one talking to a donkey? So the donkey points out the obvious. 'Hey, I'm your donkey, I don't usually act like this, so don't you think there might be a good reason?' Putting Balaam right in his place. Does God have a sense of humour? Hello! Thankfully the Angel now steps in and takes control, no doubt before the servants die with laughter.

I'm sure there are some great sitcom type scenes in the bible too. I think we almost have a Basil Fawlty moment going on with Elijah and the prophets of Baal (1 Kings 18: 16–46). I don't think God is in favour of us ridiculing other people's religions, but Elijah is obviously fired up (pardon the pun) with the Prophets of Baal and the crowd with them. He certainly gets on a roll when Baal appears unable to light the fire under their sacrificial altar. It reads like quite a rant, implying that maybe Baal can't hear them. 'Shout louder … He is a god isn't he? … Maybe he is thinking what to do? … Or maybe he is travelling? … Or busy?' That's my favourite one, 'busy', because a number of scholars imply that the literal translation is that Baal is perhaps having a toilet break; Elijah really is taking the … well, taking the mickey. Elijah finishes with 'Maybe he is asleep?' implying that Baal really doesn't care. I defy anyone to tell me that seen from Elijah's position that rant wasn't funny, although I'm sure the slightly embarrassed Prophets of Baal and their followers weren't seeing the funny side. But Elijah was doing this with a purpose; he didn't want them to have any excuses left so he gave them every chance possible. He was confident a miracle was about to happen and was making sure it was remembered; it was a well-judged comedy moment. The next bit however, is a masterful piece of theatrics that Elijah uses wonderfully to hammer home the power of his Lord. He makes their god's 'impossible' seem even more impossible by pouring water all over his sacrificial alter. He is effectively saying my God can not only do what your god can't, He can do the truly impossible, what no other can do, light a soaked altar with water spilling from the sides to create a fire that consumes not only the offering, but the stone and soil that surrounds it. He is, to put it simply, rubbing their noses in the fact. I would again have been sniggering.

When we get into the New Testament the miracles take on a much more personal tone, with Jesus suddenly in the picture, and his very first miracle has a party feel about it: turning water into wine (John 2: 1–11). From the Gospels it would appear that Jesus's mother puts him on the spot a little when she informs him the wine is all gone, to which he replies 'What are you asking me for?' Although Jesus says it is not yet his time, he can see the predicament: the wine at the wedding has run out and this isn't a minor problem. I'm led to believe that weddings in biblical times could last up to a week, so no wine left and possibly still a stretch to go is a bit of an issue. The way Jesus miraculously solves this problem must have again caused a few smirks. He has the servants top up the 'foot washing' water jars and then tells one of them to offer it to the head steward to drink. Oh yeah of course … err, fancy some foot washing water sir? All of a sudden a lot of people's faith and obedience gets tested. Not funny for them, but as a guest observer on that day it must have ignited some laughter. So, when it's confirmed as not only wine, but also the best so far, the mood must have lifted immensely and I'm sure the party quickly resumed.

Jesus seems to me to have a humorous twinkle in his eye when some of his miracles are taking place. During the 'Feeding of the five thousand' incident, or 'The miracle of the five loaves and two fishes' (John 6:1–14) for example. There is a crowd that has followed Jesus. The Bible tells us that there are 5000 men, plus women and children so it could easily be 20,000 or more people.

The disciples are obviously concerned that they all need feeding. Then Jesus says to Philip, 'Where shall we buy bread that these may eat?' Now we know he was testing the disciples, but imagine if you had 20,000 people in front of you and someone said 'Do you know anywhere where we could buy this lot a meal?' I can see the humour in that question at any time, but in the middle of nowhere and 2000 years ago! Jesus could afford to be a little lighthearted because he had the situation under control. Can you not see a smile on his face at this point?

One thing that we can't deny is that Jesus knew how to grab a crowd and get them talking. When Jesus heals the blind man (John 9: 1–12), He could have just said 'You can see' and it would have been so, but instead he spits in the dirt and makes mud to rub on the guy's eyes, and then he says 'Go wash in the pool of Siloam.' Dare I say that Jesus knew how to entertain? He was a great showman, and although much of his wit may have not made it into the gospels, I think he must have had a keen sense of humour. He is the guy who talked about Camels passing through the eye of a needle and planks in your own eye, after all. Maybe we just need to read the gospels with a more human, real, emotional, and yes, even a witty Jesus in mind?

JOHN ARCHER is an award-winning comedy magician and writer who was the first man to fool Penn & Teller on ITV's *Penn & Teller: Fool Us* and whose other TV accolades include writing and appearing alongside comedians Tim Vine and John Culshaw. He appears in the CBBC show *Help! My Supply Teacher is Magic*.

A LETTER OF SUPPORT

FROM DEREK THE CLERIC

Dear Friends

What a privilege it is for this humble clergyman to have been asked to contribute to this veritable tome and more so that I find myself in the company of so many comedic luminaries.

Whilst I am more than prepared to have a stab at lightening your countenance a tad, I am sure that the chief reason for my being included is to bring a little gravitas to the question posed: 'Does God LOL?'.

That said, I will confess to once concocting a 'gag' (as I believe it is called in the business) and it would be remiss of me to let the moment pass without recounting it. Who knows where this might lead should the likes of my fellow contributors such as Mr Ken Dodd or Mr Tim Vine chance upon my proffering and give me the proverbial 'thumbs up'?

It would surely be a feather in my cap at the local ministers' fraternal where my regular attempts to interject a spot of humour (to oil the somewhat rusty wheels of ecumenism) usually go down about as well as someone bringing a 'tongue' at St Cliff's.

Those of you who have followed my journey for some time will be aware that it was with much trepidation that I entered onto the World Wide Super Highway and I am still somewhat wet behind the ears when it comes to the popular vocabulary employed by my fellow travellers.

Thus it was my good lady wife who helpfully enlightened me as to the meaning of the appendage 'LOL' but not before I had got myself in a bit of a pickle with a message on the Facebook internet portal to old Mr McMurtry (a crusty and cantankerous member of my charge – St Cliff's).

Having given much of his time and effort to picking holes in my weekly sermons he 'messaged' my good self to inform me that my apparently erroneous theology had finally driven him to pack his proverbial bags and to seek pastures new.

Having recently preached on forgiveness (chiefly for my own benefit to assuage the ire of the fearsome matriarchs of St Cliff's kitchens after I inadvertently forgot to return a scouring pad which I purloined in the services of removing some graffiti to a sign outside our church – one particular member of my team did not appreciate the addition of the letter 'R' to the end of the warning; 'SOFT VERGE'), I had little choice but to send him on his way with my blessing (and love, or so I thought).

It was only later that I discovered that 'LOL' does not in fact stand for Lots of Love (as I had imagined) but Laugh Out Loud.

Having 'signed off' my reply to old Mr McMurtry

with the aforementioned 'LOL' (in all innocence) I was therefore somewhat surprised to find a response, by return, recanting his previous exit strategy and informing me that he was now staying put to spite me for my insensitive 'LOL', albeit it was inadvertent on my part.

It would appear that I, like St Paul, must also endure a 'thorn in the flesh' (in my case, in the guise of old Mr McMurtry).

Anyway, without further ado, here is my aforementioned 'gag'.

'Why did the chicken cross the road?'

'That is not the question rather, what on earth was the chicken doing in the story of the Good Samaritan in the first place?'

I will admit that my humour may be a little too clever for some but I trust that, with time, the penny will drop and the joke will be got.

So, to the question at hand – 'Does God LOL?'.

In that God called someone like me to be a veritable minister of the gospel I can only conclude that he most assuredly does.

Onward and upward

Derek

Post Scriptum. Should you wish to discover a little more about my good self and the goings on at St Cliff's then make a beeline for www.derekthecleric.com right away.

DEREK THE CLERIC is the creation of the writer, illustrator and popular children's author **ANDY ROBB**.

GOD JOINS THE CARNIVAL

PAUL TONKINSON

To me the fact that anything is happening at all is a testament to the fact that God has a sense of humour.

So much easier to exist in that primordial whatever it wasness that preceded space and time.

Why bring into that equation this burning, flawed amazing globe teeming with life?

What kind of artist would fashion such a piece? Was the absurdity of the notion itself motivation enough? Was the big bang the first cosmic laugh? The Ice Age a round of applause, and each of us a giggle?

And lo, into this unfurling act of creation and seeing our fallen nature God had the astounding idea of joining the carnival, becoming man, a child, living amongst us to show us the way.

The perfect example, fully human and yet fully divine. So we reach the upside down nature of revelation. A joke surely?

To the normal members of society, the true idiot the only feasible tactic would be to come in glory as a child, to be born into aristocracy, into the family of a learned man, a politician perhaps, to gain power and influence.

Hold court to the masses, overthrow emperors: triumph. Leave no doubt.

But no – God, in his infinite wisdom decided to be born in a barn, a carpenter's son. He chose to proceed humbly, to pick his disciples from amongst the unwashed, the fishermen. To eat with tax collectors, prostitutes, to judge nobody.

To tell jokes in public – blessed are the meek (What?!); the first are the last and the last shall be first (I beg your pardon!); love thy neighbour (You're havin' a larfff?!).
To heal the sick and feed the needy, throw in a few miracles on the quiet and then to be captured and offer no resistance and to descend into hell on earth and take on the collective sin of mankind and to feel the weight of that and to lose faith in God himself. Oh God why hast thou forsaken me? For God to doubt God! And then the glorious punch line, to be born again, to beat death. To offer salvation to all.

Is there a more compelling audacious story around for each and every one of us? And what to do with it?

And is it ultimately funny? Yes.

The best tactic I have found for a joyful life is to pray daily and spend a few minutes or so looking at myself in the mirror and laughing hysterically. It's only then that I am ready to meet the world.

It's easily done, I am ridiculous. My physical body, as St Francis said, an ass!

This mutinous, hairy, impractical creature that looks at me in the mirror.

And his mate, the mind – a tyrant. Uncontrollable,

repetitive, supposedly reasonable and yet inconsistent. I am a fool, my dreams ridiculous. My life a gift.

On leaving my house and venturing out the absurdities of life accumulate.

Nurses' pay. The existence of poverty, famine in a world where there is food aplenty.

Health food shops full of ill-looking people. The richest people, the poorest in spirit. Politicians who fiddle expenses accusing the newspapers of corrupt practice, who accuse the BBC of corruption, who investigate the papers' investigation of corrupt politicians. I laugh as the media eats itself. Is it not laughable? A society losing its moral parameters desperately seeking to find the moral high ground in order for its members to judge each other? And here's me judging. I told you, I know nothing, I'm a fool!

That scientists who don't believe in God spend billions searching for the God particle and then, having 'found it' realising that they have just opened the door to more mystery, wonderment.

Increasingly powerful microscopes breaking down the very stuff of life into particles, wavicles, electrons and neutrons, atoms, bosons, leptons. Matter constantly skipping away from us with a high-pitched guffaw.

That the central story of Christianity, the resurrection is embedded into the very structure of our nightly sleeping and daily awakening. Our very DNA, our cells are constantly living and dying.

That the symbol of the most ubiquitous mobile phone on the planet, a device that empowers and enslaves us in equal measures, that simultaneously propels us out into the world and directs us back into self-obsession is the symbol of the fall of man. An apple, bitten.

Everywhere you look: God the set up, and us the punch line.

It makes no sense, it makes total sense and yet like the best jokes, it's funny cos it's true.

PAUL TONKINSON is a comedian and presenter whose many career highlights include hosting *The Big Breakfast*, *Sunday Show* and appearing on *Michael McIntyre's Comedy Roadshow*. He has also been the recipient of the Time Out – Best Act of the Year award.

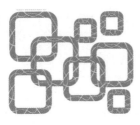

Joy is the most infallible sign of God's presence.

Leon Bloy

The glory of God is a man fully alive.

St Irenaeus

The resurrection of Christ is ... an expression of God's laughter at death, a laughter which proves infectious for human beings ... 'Death is swallowed up in victory. Death, where is your victory? Death, where is your sting?' (1 Corinthians 15:54 – 55)

Karl-Josef Kuschel

THE EDITOR REFLECTS

I'm from not only a traditional Irish Catholic background, but also a deeply-rooted show business background … if I hadn't gone into the priesthood, it would have been the *Riverdance* for me! But I've experienced some changes over my life; for instance, since wearing a dog collar, I've gotten used to a lot of people approaching me when I'm out asking 'Table for one?'

It's important that we laugh at ourselves. G.K. Chesterton said, 'Angels can fly because they don't take themselves too seriously.' A sense of humour helps us laugh at ourselves when we do begin to take ourselves too seriously. There was a true story I heard once that went along the lines of a Catholic bishop goes to visit a priest in his diocese one Sunday for Mass. The priest got up to preach the homily and began by saying, 'I'm in love with another's man's wife!' The congregation gasped … the Bishop gasped and the priest went on to say, 'I'm in love with another man's wife … I'm in love with my mother.' And then he went on to do a homily about unconditional love, while the Bishop sat there marvelling at the ingenious way he had begun his homily. Well a few weeks later the Bishop himself had to give a homily on unconditional love, and he thought to himself, I'll begin it in the same way as that priest did. He stood up in the pulpit and announced, 'I'm in love with another man's wife!' The congregation gasped ... and then his mind went blank and he forgot what came next. Then he said into the microphone, 'For the life of me I can't remember who it is now? Wait, I've got it, it's a priest in my diocese. It's his mother!'

But the irony is that when we laugh at our weaknesses and human mistakes, it highlights them and makes us aware of where we need God's strength and loving presence more in our lives. Without knowing it, sometimes our sense of humour informs us where we need to grow and the areas of our lives still to be transformed by God's power. That is one of the attributes of comedians – they highlight the frailties and misfortunes of themselves and others.

The Bible is full of these characters: comical misfits and characters the world would not entertain as modern-day heroes, yet God saw them differently and raised them up to be just that, through their foibles and idiosyncrasies. For example, here's a reflection you might know all too well but it's worth repeating:

Noah was a drunk (Genesis 9:21); Abraham was too old (Genesis 18:11); Isaac was a daydreamer (Genesis 24:63); Jacob was a liar (Genesis 27:19); Leah was ugly (Genesis 29:16–17); Joseph was abused (Genesis 37:23–24); Moses had a stuttering problem (Exodus 4:10); Gideon was afraid (Judges 6:27); Jeremiah and Timothy were too young (Jeremiah 1:4–7; 1 Timothy 4:12); David had an affair and he was a murderer (2 Samuel 11:3–4; 2 Samuel 11:14–15); Isaiah preached naked (Isaiah 20:2); Elijah was suicidal (1 Kings 19:4); Jonah ran from God (Jonah 1:1–3); Job went bankrupt (Job 1:20–21); Peter denied Christ (John 18:25–27); the disciples fell asleep while praying (Matthew 26:39–40); Martha worried about everything (Luke 10:40–42); Zaccheus was too small (Luke 19:3); Paul stood by as Stephen was stoned (Acts 22:20) and, Lazarus … well, he was dead (John 11:43–44)!

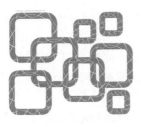

Every time you smile at someone, it is an action of love, a gift to that person, a beautiful thing.
                    Blessed Mother Teresa

Be joyful in hope.

                        Romans 12:12

This is why those whom the Lord has ransomed will return, they will enter Zion shouting for joy, their heads crowned with a joy unending; joy and gladness will escort them and sorrow and sighing will take flight.

                        Isaiah: 51:11

DID JESUS CHRIST HAVE A SENSE OF HUMOUR?

FRANK CARSON

One of the parables that I loved best of all was the Prodigal Son. He comes back from another land, and his father says to the other son, 'Go and kill the fatted calf … he that was lost is found, and he that was dead has come to life.' And so the other son said, 'Well look at me I've worked hard all my life and I've got nothing and he's blown all the dough and he's coming back you know?' And they went and killed the fatted calf because the Lord loves a sinner who repents. So at the end you'd say who most hated the prodigal son coming home? And the answer was – the fatted calf!

Did Jesus Christ have a sense of humour? Funny question to be asked, but a very serious one when you think about it.

Well personally when Jesus and all the apostles were sitting together, quite honestly I couldn't imagine them not having a laugh when they got together. When you think of the marriage feast of Cana, when Jesus was told that the wine was in short supply, he told them to bring gallons of water and he turned it into wine. Now that would have earned a worthwhile round of applause or even a standing ovation. And according to the gospel it was better than the vino the bride's old man laid on. The apostles must have had a good laugh at that and maybe they had a good hangover as well.

The miracle of the loaves and fishes would get a laugh if the Son of God, JC, were alive today. The bread and fishes would be laughed at, because the multitude would be looking for a burger and chips or a takeaway.

I can imagine one of the apostles being a funny man; there's always one in every crowd. But then if you can imagine, Jesus could not have been serious all the time. Certainly he would have had a few laughs as he answered their theological questions. Some of them may have been ridiculous, but can you imagine the Saviour of the world after addressing a large crowd and the apostles clapping like mad – and Jesus saying with a smile, 'It must be the way I tell them!' Even I laugh at that, and thank you Lord for giving me the gift of making people laugh!

FRANK CARSON (1926 – 2012) was a comedian who rose to fame through the TV programme *The Comedians* and continued to be popular through television programmes and tours all over the country. Frank received a Papal Knighthood from Pope John Paul II in 1987.

A FUNNY THING HAPPENED ON THE WAY TO THE CHURCH

ROY HUDD

This is a true story – it happened at the funeral of Danny La Rue.

The funeral was a real heavy Catholic Mass type. There were three priests behind the altar and at one point one of them, Father Christopher Vipers, addressed the congregation. He explained that Father Peter Stodart, who was to deliver the homily, was caught up in traffic and no one knew when he would get there. 'Oh well,' said Father Christopher, 'I'd better say something.' He'd hardly started when down the aisle ran Father Peter, removing his crash helmet and bicycle clips before heading into the vestry. Father Christopher breathed a sigh of relief and, casting his eyes upwards, declared, 'You see there *is* a God!' I swear I heard Danny, and the Boss Himself, laugh.

ROY HUDD is a comedian, actor and author who has appeared in many genres from television, theatre, radio and most notably, leading the cast for over 26 years in the award-winning *The News Huddlines*.

MADE IN HIS IMAGE AND LIKENESS

WILLIAM CAULFIELD

For me this has proved to be one of the most thought-provoking and soul searching questions that I have been asked in a very long time. It is a question that stirs up all sorts of emotions in me and at first glance none of them humorous. Let me clarify.

I was born and brought up in what would be classed a fundamentalist evangelical home. I have often said that I was blessed with a godly father and a praying mother whose aim and desire for their two sons was not academic success, but that they would become born-again Christians. My early memories were of Sunday School twice on Sunday, then church twice as well, children's meetings twice a week and then off to special missions as and when they were in the district. I learned there the great truths of the Bible, man's fall in the Garden of Eden, the need for salvation and the sacrificial atoning death of Christ on the cross and the need of a personal acceptance by faith to receive everlasting life.

I was taught to fear God who would judge the dead and living and to be reverential to his Holy Being. I, as a young lad of 13, became a Christian and for 17 years preached the gospel of salvation up and down the length and breadth of Ireland. Events in my life changed this, and today I find myself as a busy and successful comedian, standing before crowds of people with one desire ... to make them laugh. My Christian beliefs and bible truths are as dear to me today as they ever were, so the question does God have a sense of humour makes me re-evaluate the God I was taught to fear.

A study of the Bible reveals some 42 references to laughter and when they refer to God it is always his response to man's folly. Isn't this what a good joke is all about? The punch line nearly always involves a fall guy, the poor creature or situation we laugh at, the mirror image of God. The book of Genesis that I believe, states quite clearly that God created man in his own image and most certainly when God sent his own son into the world, born of the flesh, we can then get to see in Christ and ourselves what God is like. The Bible makes very clear that Christ experienced *every* emotion and temptation that you and I have, though he was sinless, so if I look at myself I see God. I cry, and we know Jesus wept, I sleep, I walk, I breathe, and Jesus did. I have a sense of humour, it's an integral part of me, created in the beginning in the image of God, so the God that I fear and love has also a sense of humour. Look at creation, it's full of weird and wacky things, and I'm sure God laughed and smiled when he let them loose.

Jesus on earth was not the all goody-goody that Christian fundamentalists would have us believe. He was full of wit and sarcasm; just study his replies to the Pharisees when they tried to buttonhole him, and though it's not recorded I am sure he and his disciples must have roared with laughter as they recounted the day and sat reflecting on the events. I can well believe that down deep Jesus was laughing at the devil because he knew only too well that his very purpose on earth was to defeat him and that he would.

Yes I believe that the great creator and architect of time past, present and eternity yet to come has a sense of humour; after all didn't he once strike the Philistines with haemorrhoids? (1 Kings 5:9) So when I stand in front of a crowd with a smile in my heart and see tears of laughter and the roars of joy, I will know that they are a product of my great God who has at that moment displayed a facet of his personality for all to see. Thank God for his sense of humour.

WILLIAM CAULFIELD is a comedian and actor who is a household name in Northern Ireland through his TV and radio shows, *Our William* and *It's William Caulfield*.

GOD LAUGHS!

JOY CARTER

Laughter is a beautiful complex miasma of experiences it has the power to move emotional and psychological mountains in life, encourage, educate, affect others and heal to name a few attributes. However, is the bible funny? Where and what can we learn?

My first illustration is the use of *comedy as strength in darkness* known as 'gallows humour', to overcome dire situations like the Holocaust. Similarly, some two thousand years before when Jesus was facing the final arrest in the Garden of Gethsemane we can see surprising comedy here.

It is John's Gospel account that captures much of the action describing a huge gathering of powerful local men, religious leaders and soldiers. When Jesus asked '… "Whom seek ye?" They answered him, "Jesus of Nazareth". Jesus saith unto them "I am he"' (John 18: 4–8). Immediately after saying 'I am he' everyone fell backward onto the ground under the power of God, leaving only Jesus standing. This moment is classic slap-stick comedy similar to the clowning scenes from the old black and white Charlie Chaplin films.

The sight of an angry armed mob being floored at Christ's word and not understanding why is comical.

God laughs! Imagine 1000 men in full battle dress at night getting up saying, 'What was that? Did you push me?' His mate, 'No I didn't!' 'Oh yes you did! And don't you shake your spear at me …' For people at the back of the crowd especially it must have been bedlam. Can you see it? Hilarious! Great comedy is about surprise and timing, in a split second something unexpected and funny happened against a dire background of suffering. It is the classic underdog scenario, the proud and mighty being put in their place in this scene in a pathetic heap on the floor!

Why did Jesus do it? I believe to take the edge off the unimaginable suffering he was experiencing, the suffering that was coming, and to show his great power one last time before the cross. God understands that when we face horrible circumstances in life a laugh can give us strength. Currently I am exploring 'dark comedy' in my stand up show, using the backdrop of my trans-racial adoption and the harsh difficulties I faced because of racism, bullying, cultural confusion and a lack of identity and fear. Humour is healing my heart, helping me voice unmentionable pain, educating, inspiring and freeing others through performance in this difficult, complex landscape of tangled sometimes unresolved issues. Laughter is giving me confidence to explore and express as I gradually and gently unpack memories and issues.

The book of Job demonstrates how God uses *humour to communicate* his wisdom and teaching to us. Job was a good man who God allowed to be tested as he battled rubbish friends and his own limited understanding. Comedy can create a fresh perspective in an emotional situation, thus opening our eyes to new truths. As a comedian you can learn to take a difficult situation and put it into a new context; this enables you to examine truths, heal and have fun. When Job demanded an explanation from God about his suffering the Lord answered him out of a whirlwind, which is funny yet frightening in itself (God was annoyed), but put the situation into that of a game show scenario such as Job (humankind) versus Almighty God and watch this bible story jump to life.

God starts his Q&A on Job on the premise that all his answers on basic universal knowledge would be met. Game on! Roll the comedy TV sequence. Question 1: 'Where wast thou when I laid the foundations of the earth?' (Job: 38:4). 'Eek!' thought Job, imagine him sitting in the Mastermind chair in a state of panic as he starts to realise his woeful lack of universal, scientific and omni-science as the minutes tick away and the shrill horn of a non-answer resonates again and again. Job realises and admits God's unfathomability and greatness.

I know I have questioned God a thousand times over my adoption. Why me? But reading Job helped me see things correctly as I put my adoption under a different microscope. God knows how we are made and has given us humour and biblical examples to teach us. God wasn't laughing *at* us, but through using a comedy scenario we can see the funny side as little old human beings questioning a great and mighty God! Job finally said, 'I know thou canst do everything, and that no thought can be withholden from thee' (Job 42:2). Comedy allows a person to be in the moment and yet educate and enlarge understanding in a kind and sensitive way that just telling someone would not have achieved. We can learn much from this with our relationships with each other, as humour has the power to open and engage minds in a way that intellect as a stand-alone cannot. It reaches through gender, age, intellect, class and culture and is a powerful tool in the hands of the brave and wise.

My final example is *humour in mundane life* as the Lord conspires things to make us chuckle and prove a point. Once I was in the process of finding a new church and I was inexplicably anxious about a church I had been attending for a few months. I frantically prayed, 'I need confirmation to join this church, like seeing the writing on the wall.' Now the Lord in his graciousness and sense of humour allowed me to walk into church one Sunday as the children were all displaying at the front a collage they had made of the word 'JOY'. The whole service was on the theme of joy and sure enough the 'JOY' that the children had made was put on the wall for two months. The writing of my name was quite literally on the wall: this was the church for me! It really made me LOL! God had answered my question, made me realise the folly of my worry and I could praise God for his strength when I was weak.

When we see humour in our day-to-day lives the Lord increases our capacity to learn about applying this gift, and he wants us to be at peace even in difficult situations. I am realising humour is always around if I can see it, so rather than getting crotchety and religious, I'm enjoying learning to chill out and seeing the funny side.

We should never underestimate the power of

'joy', as when it isn't evident hopelessness, despair and depression can creep in with all manner of un-pleasantness. As has already been noted, children laugh on average 200 times a day, adults only 15. As a comedian, part of the comedic process is to see things as an inquisitive child: laugh, make mistakes, get others involved, take risks, enjoy the moment and look to have fun every day! I believe joy, laughter, humour and comedy is part of our spiritual heritage not a rare treat. I am excited about learning to embrace the truths about joy and expect to go deeper into this unlimited well. If Almighty God can LOL then so should I!

JOY CARTER is a comedian, broadcaster on Sky and BBC Radio London. Joy also runs seminars on adoption and work-place comedy.

THEY WERE LAUGHING IN HEAVEN

GERVASE PHINN

I telephoned Sister Bridget, head teacher of St John the Baptist Roman Catholic Primary School (aided) to arrange for me to visit to undertake a school inspection. The nun answered the telephone with the words, 'Hello, this is the Head of John the Baptist speaking.' I suppressed my laughter and informed her that she would be receiving a visitation from OFSTED. She seemed very calm and relaxed about it and remarked that she looked forward to meeting me.

When I arrived at the school some weeks later Sister Bridget met me at the entrance. She was a slight, thin-cheeked woman with tiny, dark, darting eyes and a sharp little beak of a nose. She looked like a small hungry blackbird out for the early worm.

'Good afternoon, Sister,' I said, shaking a small cold hand.

'And did you have a pleasant journey, Mr Phinn?' she asked, her little, black, glittering eyes looking up into mine.

'Yes, indeed, Sister, a very pleasant journey.'

In the entrance hall was a life-size plaster statue

of the Virgin Mary standing on a pink cloud. She was draped in an electric blue cloak, had a golden crown on her head and carried what looked like a the sort of bomb with a fuse, the ball shaped object you see in comics. I was told this was the orb signifying Mary's position as the Queen of Heaven. The Virgin's face was smooth and alabaster white and the statue looked down upon me serenely.

The head teacher took me on a tour of the school, fluttering along the corridors, pointing and chattering and clucking away as we went from room to room. Children's paintings and poems, posters, pictures and book jackets covered every available space. Shelves held attractive books, tables were covered in shells, models, photographs and little artefacts. Each child we passed said 'Hello,' brightly and in all the classrooms little busy bodies were reading, writing, discussing, solving problems and working at the computers.

'It's a hive of activity,' I remarked.

'Does that make me the Queen Bee?' asked Sister Bridget with a mischievous glint in her shining eyes.

'May I join you in assembly this morning, Sister?' I asked her.

'Is that a rhetorical question, Mr Phinn, or are you coming in anyway?' she asked. 'I assume you school inspectors can go whither and whence you wish.'

'Yes, I will be coming in,' I told her, 'and I will sit at the back of the hall inconspicuously.'

'Oh no, Mr Phinn,' she said. 'You will sit at the front where the children can see you. Father Mullarkey, our parish priest, always sits at the front, so does the bishop, as indeed do all visitors to the school.'

'Very well, Sister,' I sighed, thinking this was going to be one school inspection I would not forget.

The little children entered the hall marching and singing loudly to the tune of, 'We are Walking in the Footsteps of Jesus' before sitting on the floor, cross-legged, arms folded over their chests and all eyes looking at the head teacher.

'Every morning, children,' began the nun, 'we have a very special visitor joining us for our assembly, don't we?'

They all chorused, 'Yes, Sister!'

'He is our dear and loving and very special friend who is always there for us. If we are naughty he is sad but he is still our friend and never turns his back on us. If we are lonely he is there to comfort us and if we want a favour he is there to help. What is the name of our very special friend?'

'Jesus, Sister!' shouted the children.

'Yes it's Jesus.' She swivelled around to face me. 'Well, this is not Jesus,' she said smiling, 'but our visitor today is Mr Phinn and he tells me Jesus is his best friend, isn't he Mr Phinn?'

'He is indeed, Sister,' I responded, forcing a smile.

'And when Mr Phinn is lonely,' continued the nun, 'he talks to his best friend, don't you Mr Phinn?'

'I do, Sister,' I said.

'And when Mr Phinn wants a favour – as when he is writing his long report about our school – he asks for Jesus' help and guidance, don't you Mr Phinn?'

I nodded. I could see the headline in the papers: 'School inspector hits nun.'

'And tell us, Mr Phinn, what words of Our Lord have guided you through your own life?' she asked, a small smile playing on her lips.

'There are so many, Sister,' I replied.

'But you must have your favourites?'

Right, I thought, I'll get her. 'Yes, Sister, as a matter of fact I do. I am particularly taken with the words of Our Lord when he said: 'Do unto others as you would hope that they do unto you.'

Sister Bridget smiled so widely that, had she been wearing lipstick, she would have left traces in her ear lobes. 'Do you know my favourite words of Jesus?' she asked.

'No, Sister,' I said, 'but I have an idea you are going to tell me.'

'Let he who is without sin, cast the first stone.'

I have an idea that the Almighty, His angels and saints were having a good laugh up in Heaven.

On my way out that day, I could have sworn that the Queen of Heaven had a smile on her lips too.

GERVASE PHINN is an award-winning speaker, educator and author, having written a host of best-selling autobiographical novels inspired by his background and former career as a teacher/education advisor and school inspector.

DOES GOD HAVE A SENSE OF HUMOUR?

CHRISTIAN COMEDIANS ANNOUNCE THEIR VERDICTS

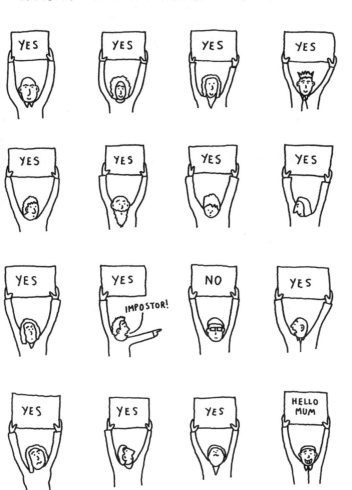

THE GOODNESS OF GOD

LIZ DAWN

God laughs? God yeah, I'd be nowhere without my faith. I've always believed in good, and if you can help somebody I think you get a good feeling, although some people never do anything, they just seem to go through life and don't even consider anybody else.

I think God helps everybody in their lives no matter how bad it is. You always find people praying when they have bad times and I think he does in some way help you to laugh at yourself or find humour in things. I think some people find things to laugh at when they're really down because it's the only way they can deal with things. Times have changed. I don't think people take each other too seriously now, it's another world, and you have so much to think about. I think that's what's good about Mass, because when you go you feel goodness and you feel Our Lord's welcome, and I can't imagine not going.
I think life goes on and I think whatever you're like on this earth you carry on in the next life, but I think you must be happier because God would want you to be happier, do you understand?

God must be funny himself ... you see when I think

of God I think of the people who die for their faith and they must have been thinking of God every hour of every day, that's how strong their faith was.

I think everybody in the Bible promoted happiness and joyfulness in their own way. I think Our Lady did; in fact she's at the side of my bed – I look at her and I just feel better. I have Our Lady and I've an angel and a crucifix and rosary beads … if anyone came in they'd think I were on my way out! Honest to God they'd think I was laid out. I have to laugh, for when I die there'll be more of them than me in the coffin.

I met Pope John Paul II once. It was quite weird really because people were taking him things at the general audience in Rome. And I took – listen to this – a statue of the Sacred Heart [of Jesus] and St Jude, and they both had hands missing and he looked at them and he blessed the Sacred Heart and St Jude with no hands and I thought afterwards – I mean he didn't show any shock he just sort of looked at them, you know what I mean, and he just blessed them. He must have thought this poor woman can't afford a proper statue! And he was fantastic … I thought he had make-up on, because his skin glowed. I just thought goodness shone out of him; it was just his face, he was a bit feeble but the face didn't show it.

Goodness and happiness shines out of God, but you can't put it into words sometimes; it's there but you don't think of it, it just happens, you know. I would be lost without my faith, honest to God. I've always prayed and felt better, and you know I find people really lovely in Church, in Mass. They always seem to have that peace, that peaceful look, especially when they've been to communion.

LIZ DAWN played the iconic character Vera Duckworth in *Coronation Street* for over 34 years, which earned her a place as one of the nation's favourite soap queens. In 2008 she was awarded the British Soap Award for Lifetime Achievement. Liz also has a MBE for her services to charity.

GOD IS A COMEDIAN

GARETH RICHARDS

The question, 'Does God LOL?' raises further questions. I think the first to tackle would be, 'Is there a God?' If the answer to that question is, 'No', then no, God does not 'laugh out loud', he doesn't do anything much, ever. I think this book is aimed at the sort of person who thinks God probably does exist, or at least possibly does exist. I would put myself in this category.

I'm the grandson of an Assemblies of God Minister. His son, my dad, was also involved in church work, and I was taken to church in the womb, and then out of the womb, and then when I was old enough that I'd forgotten that I'd ever been in a womb and the news had to be broken to me. So I'm one of those people for whom the existence of God has always been pretty much taken for granted.

I'm not sure how much God does 'out loud'. I've never audibly 'heard' anything I would definitely say was God. I don't think that thunder is God's tummy rumbling. Scientists have done tests into this and there seem to be other causes. If God did do more 'out loud' it would give the game away somewhat and make faith, well, completely unnecessary.

Laughter has a lot to do with surprise. Jokes have a twist at the end you weren't expecting, that's why you laugh at them. That's why timing is so important in comedy. You have to time the joke so the surprise has its optimum effect. It's like saying 'Boo!' to someone to scare them. So the question could be, 'Is it possible to surprise God?' This is a tricky one.

There's a lot of disagreement about the nature of God but from what I've gathered: God is everywhere, all at once, holding everything together that exists. He was always there and will always be there. Even when there was nothing, there he was. He knows everything that ever was or will be. And yet, he's chosen to create time as a way for humans to exist. He is infinite, eternal, and yet humans are, in our bodies at least, very temporal, bound by time, trapped inside it. But to make being trapped inside time more interesting he has given people free will. This is where things get complicated.

If God knows everything, then doesn't he know what choices humans are going to make before they make them? In which case how would you ever do or say anything that would surprise God? Or does he step into time with us and pretend that he doesn't know what is going to happen? Could God know and not know something at the same time? Wouldn't this be God creating a rock that is too heavy for him to lift? I've got a friend who likes to watch films he's already seen with you when you haven't seen them, and watch your reactions. I think he likes being in his comfort zone of watching something he knows he'll enjoy. I find this really annoying. Please tell me God is not like that. I prefer everyone to be having a new experience.

We must assume there are huge mysteries in the way God works, but that doesn't mean that we shouldn't at least try to understand more. Any conclusions we jump to are going to be only part of the picture, if not completely wrong, but that doesn't mean we shouldn't have a go. In that spirit ...

I think that being God is a bit like being a comedian. I'm a comedian and have met a lot of comedians, and if you know any comedians you'll know that there is an element of god-complex to our personalities. We are a people who are different from others, who have an existence and powers that normal humans do not understand.

When I go onstage I have a plan of what is going to happen. I know the routine I've prepared for this group of people and my belief is that it would be best for everyone if they just went along with my plan. If they submit themselves to my guidance, relax and enjoy the ride then that will be better for everyone. But humans are stubborn and eager to exercise their free will.

Every now and then someone will get involved with the show, by shouting something out or doing something very distracting, and my plan for the show will be ruined. However, the show must go on! I will have to adjust my plan and somehow incorporate their input into the show. If I fail to do this the audience will become disillusioned with me. The confident performer I seemed to be has disappeared and any trust that was built up will be destroyed, even though the event that caused the problem was outside of my control.

Sometimes however, the change in path makes the show much better. The sense of jeopardy adds a frisson to the gig: there was a danger that the gig would be derailed, but as the audience see me deal with the problem and keep things funny, they learn to trust me in a new way, and choose me as their guide. Although it can be nerve-wracking, when the audience interaction really goes well, those are the most joyful, brilliant gigs. And also whatever happens in the gig, you've always got in the back of your mind that you can bring things back to your planned ending.

The aim of a comedian is for the audience to have a great time, but our ability to make this happen is dependent on the open hearts of the audience.

Sometimes my jokes fall on stony ground. Somehow people have ended up at a comedy club, not really prepared for someone to come on stage and tell jokes. Or maybe they just don't like my jokes. Or maybe they just don't like me. They are closed to me.

Maybe I should have been better. Maybe I showed a lack of confidence right at the start. Maybe my jokes could have been funnier, I should have worked harder, I should have been funnier. Perhaps they just didn't feel like laughing that day because the cares of life had got them down. They just wouldn't go with me. I had done all I could for them but they just didn't open themselves up to me.

I reckon God has chosen to go with us through time.

He's everywhere all at once, but he's also right there with us. He has a plan but that plan can change and actually the interaction with us is what he's after, and what will make everything even better.

Do comedians laugh out loud? We don't laugh at our own jokes (well maybe just sometimes) because we've heard them before. We don't laugh much at jokes because we are expecting the twist, we know the shape of jokes and are no longer surprised. We are analysing what is happening. We are the people who try and make people laugh, we are not the laughers.

But every now and then something surprises us. Despite all our planning and understanding, something from leftfield catches us off-guard. Perhaps something bizarre and wonderful. Perhaps something puerile and shocking. Probably something puerile and shocking. But we are surprised and we do laugh out loud.

Like God, our ways are not your ways, but we do laugh out loud, just like you, just probably for different reasons. We are different from you, but we're also just like you.

GARETH RICHARDS, comedian and comedy singer/song writer is a Fosters Edinburgh Best Newcomer Nominee who also co-hosted the Sony Gold Award winning *Frank Skinner's Absolute Radio Show*. He has also appeared on *Russell Howard's Good News*.

GOD INVENTED EVERYTHING?

JOE PASQUALE

Absolutely, yes, he has to have a sense of humour. I went to the Vatican ten years ago after my mum died and thought about the fact that he gave people the ability to do stuff like paint the Sistine Chapel, engineers to build the leaning tower of Pisa and the Eiffel Tower and then he gives other people the power to go out and go to them.

Do you know why the Mexican threw his wife off the cliff? Tequila (to kill her).

Always remember that laughter is the best medicine … unless you're a diabetic and then insulin works better.

See what I mean? Why give one person this and then give another person that. And what is a duck-billed platypus all about? There's my answer – of course he's got a sense of humour!

God invented everything. He completely invented laughter because he had to do that. I don't understand why we're the only things that laugh. Why don't ants laugh? I don't know maybe it's just because I boil a kettle and pour it over them when there's too many of them. Generally speaking I don't understand why God only gave humans the power to laugh – although in saying that I've got a parrot and she laughs at me, but she farts as well, not with her bum! It was my dad's parrot and he farted in front of her so much that she imitates the sound and goes 'Oh pardon' and then she laughs, but I don't think she realises she's laughing. Yes he invented laughter but why he gave it to just us – I don't know.

God laughs all the time; he sits up the top there, wherever he's sitting, right on his bean bag, going, 'Look at those divs now, look at that!' I think he has the best sense of humour ever. I think he laughs at everything and he sits there and says, looking down, 'Look at what I done there, look at what's caused that now?'

I'll give you an example, just the fact that's he's given me a pilot license, me of all people. He's let me fly a plane, and I fly from Rochester over Toys R Us ... how could he actually let me, with two O levels in metalwork and biology – I can weld a car – how can he actually let me fly around the world? But he does. I think that says it all.

God's funny too but it just depends who he's with; he would be if he's with Elvis. I think at any opportunity God would have a laugh. I wonder what happens when Jehovah's Witnesses die? Do they go up to heaven and God and St Peter are hiding behind the gates going, 'Shhh, pretend were not in.' I think at any opportunity God would have a laugh – he wouldn't put laughter in the world and not know what it was himself. And not play practical jokes. I think he's got one of those squirters – I did it a little while ago I got one of those squirting things from joke shops you sit on them and it squirts water up your bum – and I think it's full of those up there!

Every time I've ever been to a funeral I've always felt this is the place now, where you need humour and the best funeral I ever went to was Bob Monkhouse's. It was a fantastic thing; if anybody had been walking past that crematorium at that time they would have wondered what was going on. It sounded like a comedy show, everybody was in fits of laugher.

Every funeral I've ever been to I've always felt that this is the time now for someone to get up there, and to do funny stories about their life, not about 'Oh no I'm gonna miss them so much …'. At my funeral (I've got in my will) that at the end, different people who are friends of mine will get up. If Bradley Walsh dies before me I've got to get up and sing at his funeral and if I die before him then he gets up and sings at my funeral. And afterwards, when it's all over, in my will I've got that where everybody has really sad music – 'Wind Beneath My Wings', 'Up Where We Belong' – I'm having a song called 'Star Trekking' played at the end when everybody's going out after I've been cremated. When everybody's going out going, 'Oh dad's gone now, what we gonna do now, he's gone forever', then all of a sudden this music will kick in: 'It's life, Jim, but not as we know it'. I think I want people to laugh, and that's when I think you need your biggest laughs then.

Laughter can break down barriers, and there's one time in particular with Wayne Dobson where that happened. I did a lot of touring with Wayne and basically, to cut a very long story short, he's got MS and he's in a wheelchair. But he still goes out and does bits and pieces when he can, at magic conventions. And I treat him exactly the same way I've always treated him, as I have known him for 20 years. I see past the disability that he has now and whenever we're out together and he has to go to the toilet, I have to take him to the toilet and all that sort of stuff because he can't do it by himself. We were up in Blackpool at a magic convention and at the end of his act, they have to put a black-out on and somebody carries him on and carries him off out of his wheelchair. I said, 'If we're going to do this we need to do it so that people aren't embarrassed by what's going on with your disability.' So at the end of his act I do this thing were I would have the music playing 'Up Where We Belong' from *An Officer and Gentleman* and he'd say, 'If life was like it is in the movies it would be a lot easier for me', and then I'd come out in the white naval outfit and I'd I throw the hat off, I'd pick him up in my arms and kiss him full on the lips as hard as I could and I'd carry him off.

We had done it a few years ago, but on this year he'd got slightly worse and had not got as much energy as he used to have; he wasn't doing as much exercise and he'd put on a bit of weight. So at the end I picked him up out of the chair but I couldn't hold him, I had to put him on the floor in front of 3000 magicians in the Opera House. I put him on the floor and the only way to get him off was to drag him off by his legs which is what I did and you know I was thinking flipping heck how can you get away with dragging a man about the floor by his legs, but I did, because it was done in the right vein and the right humour. And I sat there thinking ... if God's watching up there he must think well that was flipping funny.

JOE PASQUALE is a comedian and actor who has appeared regularly on our TV screens, including in numerous Royal Variety performances, winning *I'm a Celebrity … Get Me Out of Here!* and recently competing in *Dancing on Ice*. He has also voiced characters for Hollywood movies and performed in The Muppets' 25th anniversary show.

SERVE HIM WITH MIRTH

BOB MILLS

There was an old hymn we used to sing, when I was in our church choir:

> All creatures that on earth do dwell
> Sing to the Lord with cheerful voice
> Him serve with mirth, His praise foretell
> Come ye before Him and rejoice.

Apparently, the word 'mirth' was originally 'fear', but was changed in the Scottish Psalter, to be more in keeping with Psalm 100, which the words are based on.

I didn't know any of this at the time, of course. I was twelve. I had only really joined the choir because that gave you access to the snooker table in the Memorial Hall next to the church for a few hours after Sunday morning service, before the men arrived and turfed us kids out.

I used to sing it wrong anyway. I sang 'Him serve with myrrh' until my mate pointed that myrrh only featured in Christmas carols. So I checked in one of the few hymnals we shared, and saw it was indeed 'mirth'.

To be honest, that struck me as odd. I knew what mirth meant. It meant funny. Mirth meant Morecambe and Wise, Tommy Cooper. Peter Glaze from *Crackerjack*, fumbling through sketches with Leslie Crowther. That was mirth. What did that have to do with church? Church wasn't funny. Church was cold and serious. Church was long, interminable sermons, delivered in a thick Welsh accent. Church was struggling to stay awake, in itchy cassocks and collars.

Myrrh made a lot more sense. How could you possibly serve him with mirth? Me and my mate Ray once sang at a wedding. When the groom kissed the bride we started giggling. The boot we got under the pew from our choir master soon shut us up. Mirth? No, there was no place for mirth in church.

So ... many years pass. I leave home. Settle in a new city. I build a life. A family. Eventually, I become a comedian. I don't go to church much. I hide behind the great Protestant heresy of my own personal Jesus. I argue that I don't need a building or a formal religion to worship God. I communicate in my own private prayer. That's okay. It takes a while to realise that, in fact, congregation multiplies rather than diminishes the experience. It's all part of the learning process. As a working comedian, it's hard to be overtly religious. You work late Saturday nights. Sunday is the one day you can relax, usually. Catch up with sleep. Socialise. Also, if you work in comedy these days, religion is very, very uncool. We live in a time where, fortunately, people question certain prejudices. Jokes based on race, sexuality, and disability are all frowned on. Hopefully, we have risen above the old gags about foreigners, women and homosexuality. The problem, though, is this. Comedy needs targets. Someone has to be the butt of the joke. Surrealism is fine, self-effacement works well ... but sometimes, comedians just damn well need somebody to pick on! The rise of the *Mock The Week*-type cynical, verging on bullying performer, has created some ugly moments. Ugly people, poor people, even disabled people, have become targets. Most comics still fight shy of this, but there is one group that can be attacked easily. Religious people. Not Muslims so much: that's a bit touchy, and the Jews, well you have to be very careful, and besides, Jewish comics have that pretty much sewn up themselves. But the Christians. Wow. They are easy meat! Those crazy, mad Christians with their bizarre beliefs. The Catholic Church with its scandals and celibate men in dresses. The Anglicans with their women bishops and jumble sales. It's open season on the church. Comedy these days is full of young, educated Dawkins disciples, who have spotted a gap in the market.

'Let's take the mick out of Christians ... they have to turn the other cheek!'

Faith, of course, is a monumentally easy thing to ridicule. To believe in something so huge, based on nothing but a deep inner knowledge that it is right. It's like shooting fish in a barrel. Plus, all the things Christians are directly responsible for. Fundamentalism, war, intolerance, anything you want to pin on us really. It's a wonder we get off so lightly. Just being scorned by slim, tightjeaned young intellectual comics. I'm surprised someone hasn't come up with a night of comedy and lions.

But that's okay. We don't mind. It's harder for the evangelicals, of course, they want to argue and convert them. Save their heathen souls. Good old C of E liberals like me, we just shrug and walk away. We forgive them. They know not what they do. Of course, they do know actually. They're not stupid. They get laughs from a group of people who, by definition, don't really defend themselves. They mistake tolerance for weakness. Because we don't usually go on stage and fight back, they take this as an admission of defeat. That's cool. Most of them are our friends. We love them. That annoys them more than anything.

Also, living the life of a working comic, it's hard to stand on any high moral ground. We live amongst noise and debauchery. We mix easily with people that many would shun. We drink. We smoke. We swear. We take the name of the Lord in vain on occasions, or at least allow others to. So maybe we aren't very good Christians ourselves.

But then, sometimes, I think of that hymn. The one I didn't understand. Sometimes, I'm on stage. I set up a gag, I pause, I deliver the punch line. And then, for few moments I just watch. I watch a couple of hundred people laugh. They throw back their heads and they let go. They smile. They laugh. For a short while they forget their problems, their money worries, their pain. For an hour or so, they are happy. They aren't going to fight or argue for a while. They are just going to enjoy being.

Then I smile to myself, and think … so … this is it then, eh?

Him serve with mirth.

And the great thing is. The others … the ones who mock belief and faith … they are doing it too without even knowing.

Ha. He must LOL.

BOB MILLS is a comedian, writer and producer, whose many credits include starring in his own shows, *In Bed With Medinner* and *The Show*. He has also co-written comedy-dramas which include *Northern Lights* and *Stan the Man* and was the producer for the film *My Beautiful Son*.

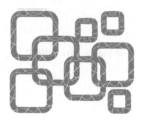

If your Jesus is boring, then your Jesus is not the real Jesus.

Dr Professor Peter Kreeft

Do not become upset when difficulty comes your way. Laugh in its face and know that you are in the arms of God.

St Francis de Sales

And all the people were overjoyed at all the wonders he worked.

Luke 13:17

THE EDITOR'S
THOUGHTS

There's an old phrase that goes, you can tell a lot about a person by the company they keep. So in order to get a closer insight into God's humour, we might learn from those who are close to him — like his ambassadors, representatives in the Church, those who spend a lot of time hanging out with him in prayer.

There was a Priest I knew in the Liverpool Archdiocese, Canon Jimmy Collins who had an incredibly popular healing ministry, accredited with a stream of miracles. He was well into his nineties when he died, only 5 foot odd and full of wisdom; he was like 'Ye Wise One'. People went to him for advice and I affectionately referred to him as the Catholic version of Yoda.

One night he was in Liverpool Cathedral conducting a packed healing service when a man with a limp approached him. Father Jimmy stretched out his hand and began to pray. The man, sensing the power of prayer, immediately stood back and in his broad scouse accent said, 'Take it easy Father, I'm on benefits!' Father Jimmy saw the funny side of that. For joy is mentioned in the Bible 244 times, and there are even occasions when

God commands his people to party and have fun. Like in Nehemiah 8:10–12 when God's people are commanded not to be sad as it's a sacred day and so they should go and enjoy themselves. Likewise in Deuteronomy 16:10–15, where the Israelites are commanded to rejoice and celebrate … but wait for it, for '7 days'. Not even stag and hen do's have that kind of stamina (though at God's do's there would be a little less alcohol consumption and those who were dressed up as angels, would literally be angels). But in this passage, God's people are told they will have good reason to rejoice as God will bless all their endeavours. As Henri Nouwen reflected, God is the God of forgiveness, reconciliation and healing, so there's a heck of a lot to be joyful about![1]

I believe those who spend their time getting to know God during their lives develop an even greater sense of humour. There's a true story about Pope John XXIII. Before he became Pope he was the Papal ambassador for France. One night he was invited to a much esteemed dinner party in Paris, and was sitting opposite a lady in a very low-cut, revealing dress. At one point during the evening someone leaned across to John XXIII and said, 'Archbishop what a scandal this is.' John XXIII who had never forgotten his humble beginnings enquired, 'What's the scandal?' To which the person replied, 'That woman in that dress, everybody is staring at her!' To which John XXIII replied, 'No one is staring at her, everybody is staring at me to see if I am staring at her.'

1. Henri J. M. Nouwen, *The Return of the Prodigal Son* (Darton, Longman and Todd, 1994).

I want to finish on this final story which is based upon some mystical visions St Philip Neri had. (He was a priest from the 1600s who was famous for his holiness and humour.) Near the end of his life someone asked him how he got to be so happy and holy. Phillip responded by saying:

At first I lived in the land of hard work until one day the angel of God came and led me to the land of silence and there I learned there was so much more to life. I slowed down and realized how much we are in danger of missing it if we are not careful. Then he came and led me to the land of love and in that land I learned the most important of life's lessons. Then one day the angel came back and he led me to the land of suffering. And there in that land the last vestiges of selfishness were purged away. And then, one day, the angel came back and he said, 'Now you Philip are ready for another land, you are ready to be taken into the inmost heart of God.' And that was the day he took me to the land of laughter.

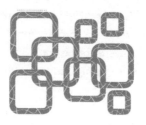

Laughter and humour are ways to prepare oneself for the ecstasy in the world to come.

Rabbi Professor Burton L. Visotzky

What are God's servants but his minstrels, who must inspire the hearts of men and stir them to spiritual joy!

St Francis of Assisi

Let the heavens rejoice and earth be glad!

Psalm 96:11

WE ARE AS GOD HAS MADE US

KEN DODD

People sometimes ask, 'Does God have a sense of humour?' And the answer is – yes. Just tell God your future plans! That's a little bit gloomy that one, but I think God does have a sense of humour. If you want proof look in the mirror in the mornings! Why have we been given this sense of humour? It's a gift, a gift to all humanity to have this wonderful facility for laughter, and a sense of humour. Do we really know what it is?

Well, in my opinion, a sense of humour is a sense of looking at things from a different angle. That is to say you have a subject there; well, instead of looking at it straight on, like we always do, try analysis; looking at it sideways, this way, that way, upside down, and you learn quite a lot about various subjects and various concepts if you just look at things differently. Very often you can look at a problem from a different point of view, and the solution will present itself right away. If you have a difference of opinion with someone, try to see it in their way as well as your way.

Sometimes it's a view that will make you laugh, because that is what humour is. It's seeing the difference in things, incongruity – perceiving the differences both of evaluations, measurements, that is what a sense of humour is and that's where and why all the laughter is created.

God has given us some of his sense of humour, God has given us this wonderful gift and it's magnificent! The gift of laughter is a tremendous Christmas present from God because it can soothe a hurt mind. It can pour oil on troubled waters, it can give you merriment, it can be uplifting and make you feel good. It's a wonderful thing, laughter!

I have many, many experiences of God's humour in everyday life; if you have the ability to see the funny side of things, it can help you every day all through your life. In fact, a very wise man once said, 'Any day in which you have not laughed has been completely wasted.' So every day is a good day if you have a good laugh.

We are as God has made us and some of us have been given various skills and some of us have been given various talents. It's wonderful the way it's all shared out. I would say every human being has some particular skill, talent, knack if you like to call it that. Everybody can do something very clever, whether it's writing poetry, singing songs, playing instruments, telling jokes, becoming a priest. Whatever it is, we've all been given various talents and we're supposed to use them for the good of everybody else.

The editor of this book is the son of a famous comedian and he must know about comedy – he's had a go at it himself – and now he's entering into another humorous vocation: giving advice to other people who don't really want it. Being a humourist, which is the same as a comedian, or a writer, being a person who loves humour, does give you a philosophical view of life. You learn to appreciate the downs as well as the ups. You can't live life entirely on the crest of the wave. You know that waves have a top and a bottom? Well, you have to learn to appreciate the view from down below as well as the view from up above.

To be an entertainer is to want to give pleasure, give a happy time to other people. The entertainers who merely do it for their own gratification, I don't think that can be very rewarding because you're only really pleasing yourself.

I get some wonderful letters. I had one yesterday and I showed it around, it was absolutely wonderful. A lady wrote to say her parents have had terrible illnesses and yet she'd bought them tickets to see my show because their favourite song was a song that I sing called 'Happiness'. I just hope we did give them another little lift, because they must be very courageous people. All through life you meet very brave people who have overcome all sorts of handicaps and illnesses. Humour and a laugh, or a song that has had a lifting effect, like 'Happiness' or 'When You're Smiling', or the songs that give you a good feeling, are very important.

In the Bible there is one quotation that used to puzzle me. 'Laughter is like the crackling of thorns.' Yes, but it's like setting fire to the crackling of thorns underneath a cooking pot.

Laughter can be destructive; it can be just personal gratification, if that's all that's behind it. The best kind of laughter is when you make somebody else happy and make somebody else's life a bit better. And surely that is God's work. God doesn't want us to be miserable, I'm sure. God doesn't want us to be going round all the time beating our chests and bemoaning and whingeing. I'm sure God wants us to be joyful! And enjoy each other's company … and enjoy each other's laughter and joy!

I hope there will be laughter in heaven. There are people who say there isn't, but I'm sure there's joyful laughter in heaven. If you want to hear the most beautiful laughter, surely the kind of laughter you'll get in heaven, pass any school playground and you'll see little children jump up and down, leaping around, and laughing, laughing. Why? For the sheer joy of being alive! No jokes, no funnies, just for the sheer joy of life! The beautiful feeling you get when the sun is shining and you go out one morning and you breathe that lovely, beautiful clear air and you think 'God, it's good to be alive.'

Life as a comedian, I'm sure, has helped me enormously. I'm positive it's helped me to stay alive as long as I have done. I think a happy heart does help you, oh yes, I'm sure it helped me. I can't think of a time when I didn't laugh. Even when things haven't been going all that great, I've still found something to laugh at. The perception or the view of other human beings, the things they do and the way they behave is quite comical; yes it does make you laugh!

My favourite person in the Bible is obviously Jesus. I don't say he was a stand-up comedian but he told the parables and some of them are quite humorous. Certainly they perceive the inequalities and the un-equal ness of human nature and its frailties. They're great stories and some of them are very whimsical.

You see a comedian really is a communicator, as well as being just a gag teller or a joke teller and pulling funny faces. Basically at the very core of his being he is a communicator of ideas hopefully comical ideas; hopefully, ideas that will get a laugh, particularly if you tell it the right way. I do really admire anybody who can communicate thoughts in a very, very strong and efficient manner. So, therefore, probably the greatest communicator of all must have been – Jesus Christ!

KEN DODD is a comedian, singer/songwriter and actor, having appeared in a vast array of television programmes from his own shows to Royal Variety performances, with past regular UK chart success. Ken once held the record for not only the longest comedy performance, but the record for the longest running comedy show to have played the London Palladium. Ken Dodd OBE is a national treasure!

ABOUT THE CARTOONISTS

ROBERT DUNCAN specialises in cartoons for advertising. He has worked for almost everyone, including Coutts & Co, Abbey National, Kodak, American Express, Hotpoint, Sir Tim Rice and lots more. He has produced over 3000 greeting card designs, including the world famous Not Particularly Orange range.

MYCHAILO KAZYBRID has worked professionally in the cartoon and comic book industry for over 37 years, mainly on licensed characters and titles, including Wallace and Gromit, Shaun the Sheep, Duckula, Dangermouse and Bash St Kids. His other work includes nine years producing daily cartoon strips for provincial and national newspapers, the production of international comic strips for mobile phones, and four years in broadcast television.

SIMONE LIA began painting and drawing in her Dad's tool shed at the age of 13. Since then she has gone on to write and illustrate books for children, set up an art studio in an old pub, and written graphic novels, including *Fluffy* and *Please God, Find Me a Husband*. Her characters include a wilful sausage, a carrot, a chip who doesn't speak and bunnies of various shapes and sizes.

DAVE WALKER is a freelance cartoonist. Best known for his church-themed cartoons, he now draws cycling-themed cartoons too. His weekly cartoon, 'The Dave Walker Guide to the Church', featured in the *Church Times* for seven years.

MARY'S MEALS

Mary's Meals is a global movement that sets up school feeding projects in some of the world's poorest communities, where poverty and hunger prevent children from gaining an education.

Our idea is a simple one that works. We provide one daily meal in a place of learning in order to attract chronically hungry children into a classroom, where they receive an education that can, in the future, be their ladder out of poverty.

The Mary's Meals campaign was born in 2002 when Magnus MacFarlane-Barrow visited Malawi during a famine and met a mother dying from AIDS. When Magnus asked her eldest son Edward what his dreams were in life, he replied simply: 'I want to have enough food to eat and to go to school one day.'

That moment was a key part of the inspiration that led to the founding of Mary's Meals, which began by feeding just 200 children in 2002. Today, just over a decade later, we feed more than 730,000 hungry children every day in 16 different countries across the world, including Kenya, Haiti, Uganda, Liberia and India.

Our work is named after Mary, the mother of Jesus, who brought up her child in poverty. We consist of, we respect and we reach out to people of all faiths and none.

The average worldwide cost for us to feed a child for a whole school year is just £10.70 (or 6 pence per meal). Wherever possible, Mary's Meals uses locally grown food to support the local economy. We work hard to keep our running costs low and to ensure that at least 93 pence of every pound donated to us goes directly on our charitable work. This is only possible since most of our work is done by an army of volunteers.

All over the world, there are people who will not accept that any child in this world of plenty must endure a day without a meal. As a result of the good deeds of our supporters and volunteers, thousands of children, who would otherwise be working or begging for their next meal, are instead sitting in a classroom with a full stomach, learning how to read and write.

With 300 million chronically hungry children in the world, our work is just beginning. Our vision is that every child receives one daily meal in their place of education. Working together with those who share our ideas, we believe there is no good reason why this vision cannot be realised.

Support for Mary's Meals is global, with fundraising and awareness-raising groups springing up all across the world, in such countries as Canada, Australia, Austria, Bosnia and Herzegovina, Croatia, France, Germany, Italy, Netherlands, Portugal, the United Arab Emirates and the United States.

www.marysmeals.org